I Am Who I Am Because I'm Not Who I Was

THE AUTOBIOGRAPHY OF LAMONT TAYLOR

BY

LAMONT TAYLOR

"The how is never as
important as the why"

Printed in the United States of America

First Edition, 2023

HARDBACK ISBN: 978-1-0881-2257-0

PAPERBACK ISBN: 978-1-0881-2289-1

EBOOK ISBN: 978-1-0881-2289-1

Red Pen Edits and Consulting

www.redpeneditsllc.com

Disclaimer

Some names have been changed to protect and respect the identity and privacy of some people. Language and situations reflect the authenticity of a life well-traveled and deep rooted in raw experiences.

TABLE OF CONTENTS

CHAPTER ONE

Momma's Boy   1

CHAPTER TWO

Lifelong Lessons Of Middle School   12

CHAPTER THREE

This Teenager Got It All Figured Out   42

CHAPTER FOUR

From Stupid Teenager To Military Man   76

CHAPTER FIVE

The Rollercoaster Of Life Is A Bit Overwhelming   136

CHAPTER SIX

The Example Of Change: Becoming A Successful,
Proud, Black Business Man & Leader   187

ABOUT THE AUTHOR

Lamont Taylor   225

ACKNOWLEDGEMENTS

(People Who I Love, Supported Me, Inspired Me,
Or Encouraged Me Along The Way)   231

Dedication

This book is dedicated to my parents, Irene and Willie

Taylor.

To my beautiful and supportive wife, Tasha.

To my daughters Ayanna Taylor, Kyra Johnson, Laila

Mack.

I thank all of you for being my support system and my

purpose.

You are the real reason I Am Who I Am!

I love you all . . .

Family Vacation In Upstate New York

Our First Family Portrait As A New Family

Chapter One

MOMMA'S BOY

The busyness of the Raleigh-Durham International Airport is one I've grown accustomed to, but it rarely bothers me. I've flown in and out so often that travel is second nature. Ironically, growing up I always wanted to be a traveling businessman. Didn't matter the business I just wanted to travel the world on planes with a briefcase looking important. However, after the first dozen or so flights it becomes tiring and overrated. Escaping to a sunny destination soothes the soul, especially for a black man who grew up working the tobacco fields in the Tar Heel state. However, I'm not looking for comfort. The dozen or so trips to the Bahamas are all about business, and I'm always about the grind.

Motivation pushes me during the day and keeps me up at night. Most of the cats I know just don't have it in them. Trust me, your boy has enough of it to go around, and I'm willing to share it if you're ready to accept all that comes with riding with me, Lamont Taylor. My appearance and getaway destinations might look glamorous, but getting here was all about survival. My road to purpose has had many detours.

***

Black Santa Visit In NYC

Brooklyn In The House

In 1972, Irene Taylor brought me into the world, and the unknown difficulties of life started right from the jump. My body wasn't ready to handle the transition from womb to fresh air, so the doctors rushed me out of the delivery room to save me. My mother had to wait weeks before she could see my face and breathe love into her baby boy. Kings County Hospital in Brooklyn, New York, was my beginning, and thankfully, the doctors knew what they were doing. They went to work ensuring that my life could have moments of success, and I proved how strong I was built right out of the gate.

My parents took me home to our duplex in Brooklyn at 194, Tapscott Street. The early years of my life were spent in and out of the hospital. My tiny body held up during corrective surgery to fix the crossed eyes and heart murmur I was born with. Then, medical professionals fit my legs for braces so I could learn how to walk properly. My asthma was so severe that I damn near lived in a bubble for a few weeks so I could develop and the hospital could run tests. The back-and-forth trips to regulate my breathing would continue for a few years as I spent so much time fighting for air. Even now, there are times I have to reach for my inhaler.

A rough start is where I probably earned my childhood reputation for being stubborn. Who wouldn't develop such a trait with so many odds stacked against them? I was told there were many times when we would eat out as a family, and I would sit right there as my parents enjoyed the cuisine. The food could've been from the best soul food joint or every kid's favorite at the time, White Castle. It never mattered to me. I would refuse unless we went to my favorite pizzeria. You weren't going to tempt me with anything else, and I would hold out for hours to show the seriousness of the situation. My mother always marveled at my willingness to stand my ground as a child. It was preparation for greatness and some future, foolish activity.

Those early struggles also made me fearless, well at least to a point. To this day there are still three things in life that can really get me shook. I don't like the whirling winds of a tornado, slithering snakes, and evil little mice. Yeah, I said it. I am afraid of mice. My mother is to blame for me losing control at the sight of a mouse. One of those creatures once got inside our duplex, and I joined my mother on the bed, jumping and screaming like a little girl. In fact, it was my cousin, James Earl (R.I.P.) who had to save us from the beady-eyed bandit. So, you get a clear picture of the seriousness of this fear. There was a moment, as a grown man, that I went on a rampage in my own house, shooting at a mouse with a gun. Whatever, don't judge me.

We stayed in that old duplex until I was about five, and that's when we moved down to Proctorville, North Carolina. It was home for both my parents. My father actually used to be my mother's bus driver. But before you cancel my father as some kind of perv, you have to remember this was a time when they used to let teenagers in school drive the bus. Yeah I know, crazy huh? Brooklyn will always hold a special place in my heart. It's where I learned the fight in life starts within. But deep down I was meant to be a down-south country boy.

Unconditional Love

Irene's Son

I understood North Carolina wasn't New York. Some roads had dirt, and trees blanketed the landscape for miles. An unfamiliar sound occupied the night and early morning. It was strange to trade in loud automobiles and teenagers on a stoop, for crickets chirping, but the quiet and safety compared to the 70's streets of New York City was something my parents wanted for their only son.

The house in Proctorville was different from anything I had ever experienced before. Yes, I was only five, but I knew Brooklyn had indoor plumbing. That's not something a kid could easily forget. Imagine having to use the bathroom in a white bucket, then having to take it outside to dump it in an outhouse. Yet the kids today have the nerve to complain. Talk to me about complaints when you've emptied a bucket of piss and stankin poop in an outhouse a few times. I don't know what was worse; the smell or the flies.

We spent four or five years in that house, and it wasn't all bad. My best friend was with me, and we did everything together. He was a German Shepard named Sarge. Being an only child, you have to have a vivid imagination and a pet. I loved Sarge so much I swear he could talk. At least I would like to think he could, considering I was always talking to him.

During one of those rare snowy winters, I remember not seeing Sarge come to the door when we opened it. He always came to the door. I called his name, but Sarge never appeared, so my father went looking for him. He pulled him out from underneath our house, and my best friend was frozen stiff as a surfboard. I blamed the weather for freezing him to death. Years later, I realized that the temperature was never cold enough to snatch Sarge's life. The stiffness was rigor mortis setting in. That was my first traumatizing experience with death, but it wouldn't be my last.

I've always had a special bond with my mother, perhaps because I'm an only child. My parents tried for another baby when I was four, but she was stillborn. They named her Vanessa, and my mother says it broke her heart when I refused to leave the hospital until they gave me a sister to take home.

Losing Vanessa and dealing with my ailments during those early years caused my mother to hold on to me as tight as possible. Some might say I was spoiled, but I believe she offered me the extra love she couldn't give to my little sister. Make no mistake about it, everyone in town knew I was Irene's boy, Lamont and how she felt about me. The extra love that she gave me was only one way I was special. There were many children in town who came from broken homes. I had two loving parents at home, which was a rarity I appreciated more than I showed then, and that I appreciate even more now.

I recall we had something called May Day at Proctorville Elementary, and they always produced the prestigious brag worthy King and Queen of the Court. Students didn't vote to see who would earn the honor. A candy bar selling system determined the royal winners, and your boy won King every year of my elementary career. I won because my mother sold candy bars to the customers she served at her restaurant job as a waitress. She made sure her baby sold the most. I remember a few teachers said, "We're glad Lamont is leaving because now someone else can win King of the Court."

My mother has reminded me a time or two of an instant that she never forgot. It was one of those years after winning King, as everyone was finishing up the festivities, she bought me a hot dog. Having rushed there from work to see me crowned, she asked me for a bite but I refused. Man how that must've hurt her feelings. A parent myself now, I know all too well how children can be cold and hurtful. I really wish I could change that memory, along with many others I suppose. I have always regretted that selfish act. It's quite shameful.

My Mother, Irene

After Sarge, Shawn Graham became my human best friend. We met in kindergarten and stayed close throughout our elementary years. We would race up and down the road and play basketball together. If I was into something, you could bet Shawn was right with me, whether it was good or bad. He helped me settle in at school and made those elementary years memorable.

Shawn was there in the second grade when Ms. Walters slapped me across my face in the back of the class. Shawn must have felt the pain because he turned his head away from Ms. Walters as soon as her hand connected with my face. I don't quite remember what I did to get slapped, but I knew it wasn't over. Remember, everyone knew I was Irene's son, so you knew she wasn't going to be OK with her baby getting assaulted. Sure enough, she showed up. Willie and Irene Taylor played their roles. Daddy never pursued confrontation, or at least once he became a family man. I've heard the stories of the Taylor boys, my father and his brothers, who would terrorize anyone who challenged them. But my mother, on the other hand, was about that life. You couldn't think about making some mess to her family and expect it to slide. My daddy pretty much supported whatever and however she decided to handle things, including disciplining me. I had only received one beating from my father, so you know that one time I must have done something terrible. Anyway, Ms. Walters' slap brought my mother to school, and she let it be known that anyone not named Irene Taylor better keep their hands off of Lamont.

Chapter Two

LIFELONG LESSONS OF MIDDLE SCHOOL

Middle school at Fairgrove came with many lessons and a few teachers who left their mark. Mr. Lesane was one who taught me a thing or two. He knew my Uncle Lee from back in the day. It turned out that they were the best of friends. Mr. Lesane was a strong, dark-skinned brother with a clean, shaved head. He was approachable on a daily basis, but he wasn't about that bullshit. You could puff your chest out if you wanted, but best believe that teacher would deflate your ego with a quickness.

These new school cats don't know how rough we had it when class was in session. ISS (In School Suspension) or being put in timeout had nothing on getting touched-up by one of those woodshop paddles. Mr. Lesane's two-foot-long custom paddle had holes drilled in it that would capture the wind to help pick up speed before impact. I still have nightmares about that thing.

Mr. Lesane had warned us multiple times to stop talking in class one day, but I ignored his warnings, hoping that he wouldn't lose his cool.

"Mr. Taylor," Mr. Lesane said.

A whisper would've been too loud, the way his tone silenced the classroom. I could choose to ignore him mentioning my name or take the next step in sealing my fate. "Yes sir?" I asked.

"Front and center," Mr. Lesane said.

As much as I loved talking, I never enjoyed negative attention. It was the kind of embarrassment you carried for weeks. The march up front seemed like an eternity, and with all eyes on me, I even began to sweat a bit. My hands pressed against the desk as I braced for impact. The pain was harsh, but I didn't cry. Your boy was too cool to be up there crying in front of all the girls. A boy has a rep to protect. Mr. Lesane always said he wouldn't hit us if he didn't love us. I only wish the brother didn't love me so much at that moment.

Uncle Lee thought the paddling was hilarious. Irene didn't show up at the school that time. When you're right you're right, but when you're wrong you're wrong.

Next up was my 5th grade teacher Mrs. (Mary) Davenport. There was never a teacher as strict as her, and I'm glad about that. We needed someone like her to push us and teach us. Mrs. Davenport used to say, "I can't make you do anything you don't want to do, but I can make you wish you had." I never received a paddling from her, because I learned my lesson by watching her swing. Mrs. Davenport could've played for the Yankees with that swing in motion. She beat the dust off that ass, never striking out.

Mrs. Davenport's class wasn't as bad as some kids said. She was the kind of teacher who offered support in the classroom. Some of the best-looking girls were in that class, like Scarlett. Scarlett Locklear was a little Lumbee Indian (Native American) girl with a beautiful personality and an absolutely gorgeous face. She knew how to make fun out of every moment. I got to school one day, and Scarlett was noticeably missing, and Mrs. Davenport wasn't at her desk monitoring the class. We knew better than to horse around in her absence, so we sat in our seats, waiting for class to begin. Mrs. Davenport slowly entered along with the principal. I could tell something was off. They told us that Scarlett was in a car accident that left her dead. Her body flew through the windshield on impact . . .

That day marked the first time I lost a friend to death. Thoughts of Scarlett continue to cross my mind to this day, and her untimely exit signals the struggle I've had with dealing with death. I think my obsession or fear of death all circles back to the beginning with Scarlett. I mean, back then there was no grief counseling for kids. We just were allowed sometimes to cry in class. She and so many others missed out on what could've been. It all haunts me. Like Nas said, "I never sleep cuz sleep is the cousin of death."

Another Mrs. Davenport's incident that stands out in my memory had to do with social class. It's a lesson they teach us so early in life, and most of the time, we don't even notice. You got the kids who have packed lunch or pay full price, the kids who have reduced priced lunch, and the kids who are on the free lunch program. I was on the reduced list, so I still had to show up with some money for lunch. One day, I forgot my lunch money, and the lesson was to sit at the table with Mrs. Davenport and watch the other kids eat. My mother wondered why I was starving after school.

"Boy, why are you acting like you didn't eat lunch?" Mom said.

I exhaled and put extra emphasis on my words. "That's cuz I didn't!" I said.

I only wanted my mother to give me something to eat because I was hungrier than usual. The last thing I wanted was for her to kick in the school's doors and let them have it. A parent having your back is fantastic, but I didn't want the smoke she could create. After all, I had to play the role of the student each day. But, Irene didn't play about her baby, especially when it came to not being fed. I mean, who could blame her? Any of us would be smoking mad if one of our kids was denied food. So my mother and I went to the school for a meeting with Mrs. Davenport and the principal. My mother firmly explained that she would've paid the money back if they had given me food.

"We're talking about a 10-year-old who forgot his money.

People would at least give a dog a bone," Mom said.

I see where Mom was coming from, but I sincerely didn't think and still don't think my teacher meant any harm. I tell you what, forgetting my lunch money was never an issue again. One time of going without food taught me to never do that again. Nowadays, schools make sure students get fed no matter what, but they make sure parents pay back what is owed. It's how things should be.

My mother understandably never really cared for Mrs. Davenport after that day. I, on the other hand, was more forgiving. Mrs. Davenport was one of my favorite teachers and even now we're Facebook friends. I stopped by to see Mrs. Davenport and her husband, Mr. Jackie, at their house about five years ago. Now, I can't say Mr. Jackie was one of my favorites when I was in middle school. He coached basketball, and everyone, except him, knew my skills were good enough to make the school team. But Mr. Jackie's eye for talent was obviously not up to par.

I was what the department stores called "husky" back then. Middle school is tough on kids, and your confidence can take a devastating hit. Mr. Jackie cut me from the team while the popular boys like Tony and Rodney made the squad. I played with those boys, and they all knew I had good enough skills on the court. It became the single most disappointing basketball moment in my life. Thanks, Mr. Jackie. I never made the team in middle school, but it would help shape me later in life. I mean, I think that situation made me the most competitive person on earth. I never wanted to lose again. Never left room for doubt. And besides, I forgave Mr. Jackie a long time ago for being wrong.

Clapping increases with a thunderous sound as the roars intensify. The noise isn't coming from the stands, nor is it the result of good decision-making. The five-person team with Darius at the one is down by 10 points, but the young male diva has an astonishing 36-8-5 stat line. The amazement has to do with zero assists making up those numbers, and his teammates have had enough. They're barking at him to share some of the success, but he can't see the forest from the trees.

Too much of Darius' play has centered around his "me first" approach. A sixth steal gives him the ball with a defender on his left and one in front. The ball goes through his leg as his left hand quickly flicks it forward through the same route while his teammates continue to clap, signaling that they're open. Darius executes the killer crossover as he glides to the basket for an easy layup.

"There's no I in team, Darius," one of his teammates said. Darius shakes his head. "No, but there's an M-E."

The heat from the sticky gym can't equal the boiling level my nerves have reached. We sub out Darius and place him next to me at the end of the bench. My approach can't match his same level of disrespect, or I'll lose him, and the boy is too talented to let him mess up an opportunity that can put him on a path to purpose. The moment for mentorship and counseling had arrived.

"Individual success is important, but not at the expense of your teammates," I said.

"I'm embracing the Mamba Mentality," Darius said. "Kobe said the same thing to his team."

"Do you think Kobe won those championships by himself? He didn't become the Lakers' second all-time assists leader playing by or for himself," I said. "You can't be the best you without involving the other guys."

"Everyone's just a bunch of haters," Darius said.

The young man didn't understand the situation he had created. Darius thought the others were jealous, but in reality, they didn't like his selfish style of play. On the flip side, the opposition, who should be the haters, had no respect for his game.

"Listen, middle school is the time when you start forming bonds with some of your peers," I said. "Some of these guys will be with you during tournaments and camps throughout the next four years." When someone talks about haters, I know what that's about. Those types of people naturally fall in line when you do what is necessary to earn the respect of others. The haters don't like when you garner such attention. Darius hadn't reached that level because he wasn't ready. However, sitting his ass on the bench and watching his squad bite into that lead would show the brother a thing or two. I remember when my showmanship introduced me to the feel-good respect of the crowd and the hate that followed.

A move across the way before middle school drew me from my day one friends. Everyone knows that middle school is a tough time for adolescents. Some call seventh grade, 'the year of the jerk.' I had to get used to seeing my old friends during the occasional visits to the old neighborhood, but my personality wouldn't allow me to go without in the meantime.

The North Carolina heat stuck to my skin like a shadow during the summer of 1984. Luckily, I didn't have to travel far before I found someone else to share the burden of the sun. A few houses down was a couple of guys in the neighborhood named Dexter and Marlowe who moved down from New York City. Dexter was a few years older and Marlowe was closer to my age, and new to Fairgrove Middle School. We quickly became good friends. He was a heavy guy, but his confidence didn't allow his weight to handicap the person he wanted the world to see. Marlowe was that cool cat who embodied the culture of New York City without throwing it in your face. The boy was fresh to def from his b-boy style, to his DJ skills. It made sense for our coolness to come together as best friends. I showed him how we got down in the south, and he shared his NY influence.

We spent the summer listening to Afrika Bambaataa, Rock Steady Crew, Whodini, Big Daddy Kane, Run D.M.C., and my favorites, Eric B. and Rakim, and Public Enemy. Lyrics echoed across the neighborhood while we walked the country road, blasting our generation's identity. More kids joined in, creating bonds that weren't forced and didn't require specific threads. Marlowe was always going to have that new gear because that's how he carried his swagger from the boroughs. I was never into keeping up with the Joneses, so shelled-toe Adidas, four-finger rings, and Lee striped pants didn't satisfy my needs. Being me was enough for the cool kids, girls, and everyone else. I could play ball with the jocks and rock with the misfits all on the same damn day. When I say misfits, I'm not talking about the knucklehead troublemakers. These were the guys who weren't getting any play from the homegirls and didn't have representation in the cool kid crowd. If you're confident in yourself and show the world a little of who you are, then something has to give if you're patient. I've always just been confident in who I am. Love me or not, I'm me.

I always received good grades and awards in middle school.

Being the guy who lived in two different worlds in school didn't interest me. I would walk the path of notoriety by speaking with ease to the cool bunch but gravitating toward the misfits. They were going to make themselves known because I couldn't let them fail at the popularity game. Flyers for the school talent contest at the annual May Day celebration had circulated around the halls. Kids were willing to impress their peers with singing, dancing, and rapping. As middle schoolers, we weren't the most innovative group, so most went with what they knew. Students were practicing their Prince, Tina Turner, and Billy Ocean routines in the bathrooms. Fellas, who had semi-decent voices and moves teamed up for their best New Edition, 'Cool It Now' performance. I knew Marlowe had the classic New York hip- hop dance moves, like pop-locking and the knee spin, so pairing up with him was a no-brainer. However, the fly guys had the same idea, and they got to my friend before I could deliver my pitch.

There wasn't any jealousy involved. I knew Marlowe had a great chance to showcase his skills to the entire school to see if he got with the right people. I decided to crew up with the misfits and form a pop-locking group. Mike Bethea, Mike Oxendine, and I went to work honing our craft. One thing I wasn't going to do was embarrass myself on stage. I spent days watching *Soul Train* reruns, *Beat Street* and *Breakin'* to perfect our movements. The show had a lot of people doing their best to make a statement. Crewed up and ready to go, the crowd started hollering as we inched toward the center circle. Unfortunately, I could clearly see why. Marlowe stood center with Tony Paylor and Rodney Glover. Like I said, Marlowe got with the right guys. You had to wear sunglasses in the presence of Tony and Rodney, or their coolness would blind you. They were the ballplayers who invented the term panty dropper. To make matters worse, they knew Marlowe was the icing on the cake. His rerun showmanship with the New York grit was everything.

Following Marlowe, Tony, and Rodney would be ego-deflating for anyone, but I knew then that if one thing was true, I was Lamont. The beat got those heads bobbing and those necks rolling as we made an appearance. My guys were smooth with it, and I had all the flair of Whodini's Ecstasy. We popped and locked to 'Five Minutes of Funk' while the girls screamed, and the homies chanted. Our arrival was unexpected, but it couldn't be denied that we had placed ourselves in our own popular zone.

We had the crowd, but hey, school is about cliques, so we didn't win. Anyone who didn't know Lamont before knew me then, and the two Mikes now had skin in the game. The new status raised my level, but it wasn't always about the good. The haters showed up on time. One such hater turned out to be Fat Cat (I don't remember his real name). My area was dominated by the Lumbee Tribe of North Carolina, and Fat Cat was a member. Our school was 45% black, 45% Lumbee Native American, and 10% white. At this time, Fat Cat was a beast of a manchild, towering at 6' 8" and growing (somehow, he shrunk to a modest 6' 0" by our adult years). He was the bully who looked like he ate the bully sitting next to him. He ran the school along with another bully, Bill Seals.

Kids came up to me saying that Fat Cat was on the hunt, and I was his target. Remember, I'm the guy who gets along with every group, but now I had a target on my back, and I wasn't quite sure why.

Fat Cat stomped toward me at recess and said, "I'm gonna beat your ass, Lamont."

"What's wrong with you?" I asked.

I'm no punk, and I wouldn't back down from this man-boy. I'm intelligent, so fighting a dude who looked like he ate rocks for fun didn't seem the best strategy. I had my reputation with the ladies to protect, so damaging it in a fight with nothing to gain was counterproductive to my future player. Middle school fights generate buzz, so the crowd multiplied quickly. We squared up as the other students amped up their excitement.

In a moment of clarity, I leaned into Fat Cat. "We're gonna fight, but come here so I can talk to you first," I said. We went around the corner, and I hatched a plan. "Everyone thinks we're going to fight. Wouldn't it be cool if we acted like we were but then didn't and fooled everybody?"

Fat Cat stared me up and down but decided that my approach would be kinda funny. We moved back toward the other students and took our positions. We circled the invisible ring as if we were Sugar Ray Leonard and Roberto Duran.

"Are y'all ready for this fight? I'm about to beat his big ass," I said, hoping I didn't go too far and hit a nerve and offend him.

The crowd believed we had bad intentions. Fat Cat squared up with me, but I couldn't tell if he genuinely bought into my playground politics. He could've decided to let one go and end my reputation at any moment. When I thought Fat Cat will swing, he threw his hands up, and I did the same.

"There's not gonna be a fight here today, so take y'all asses on" Fat Cat said.

Our fellow students looked disappointed and confused as Fat Cat and I walked off the playground arms on each other's shoulders. I learned that day that I have the gift of the gab and could use it to pull respect from the most feared haters.

Looking back, there wasn't one time during the start of middle school when I allowed my ego to outshine my boys or bring jealousy toward Marlowe for doing him. They'll respect you if you do it the right way. That attention will invite the haters, but legit haterism doesn't exist without respecting something about the other person.

Middle school had its ups and downs, but it was clear that I had arrived. However, popularity and dealing with bullies weren't the only lessons I had to learn. Somewhere in the mid-80's, some of the teachers took a group of us to watch *The Color Purple* as part of a field trip. I suppose you read the book or viewed the film. In that case, you know the story tells a darkening truth about the racial divide in our country and how prejudice manipulated the African-American community into turning on each other. As kids, we didn't know anything about the movie other than it was black, and we got to miss school. It was a perfect teaching moment opportunity, but only if our educators would've realized we needed one. Outside of munching on popcorn and drinking soda, I remember Celie getting busted upside her head with a rock. At the time I thought it was hilarious and had no real historical significance.

How can you take a group of black and Indian kids to a significant emotional film and fail to ensure they leave with an understanding that will force them to question everything? It was almost as if the teachers used us to get their desired entertainment. Certain moments in life provide opportunities to educate people before they experience types of prejudice. We weren't prepared for the life we would face. We had no idea how much that film could've helped us prepare and deal with the residual tragedies of American history we would have to ultimately deal with.

I was riding my bike to a friend's house when I was about twelve years old. We lived out in the country, so any distance between points a and b could be a few miles, but I'll be damned if it didn't feel like twenty miles, as hard as it was to peddle that bike. I spotted a little Indian girl playing by herself in her front yard. She was having the time of her life, but she froze as I started to pass her house. The little girl stopped what she's doing and hurried to the edge of the ditch in her yard.

"N-I-G-G-E-R," she yells. Her eyes follow me as I breeze by.

Why would she say that? Who am I to her? Indeed it was a mistake.

"Nigger, nigger, nigger," she yelled again.

I'm not a nigger. I'm Lamont, but I was the only person around, so the girl had to be talking to me with her learned hate. It was the first time I remembered being called a nigger, but this is America, so it wouldn't be the last. I rode my bike home to tell my mother what had occurred. There wasn't any fear or anger, but curiosity troubled my mind that day. It still does. Over the years, I would ride my bike and then drive my car past that house. I still do.

Did that little girl stay and inherit the property? Is she a grown woman living in that house thinking about the black boy that used to ride by? She doesn't know that her racist antics are stuck in my mind and continues to live there almost forty years later. There's a process, an unwanted badge of courage that black people have to go through in this country. My white brothers and sisters can empathize, but they will never understand. It's an uneasy feeling of always being looked upon in a negative way. Even when you may not be judged at that moment you still feel you are. You can never shake it. It consumes your mind from the first time you are called nigger. You don't know if there's anyone who's not black that you can trust.

My parents understood I needed an escape from the south, so each summer, I went back to Brooklyn to stay with my favorite aunt and uncle. Aunt Adell and Uncle John were the absolute best, and I looked at them as an extension of my parents. Their place was in Coney Island, a peninsular neighborhood in Brooklyn, and it was off the chain during the summer months. Their spot was on Ocean Avenue across from the boardwalk and amusement park. There was too much fun to keep to myself, so my cousin Anthony was always there with me. I always looked forward to getting back to New York.

One of my fondest memories of visiting New York, when I was just a young boy around nine, consisted of a summer concert at the Mecca, Madison Square Garden. Aunt Adell and Uncle John's daughters, Diane and Clairdell, took me to my first concert. Frankie 'Hollywood' Crocker, the famous DJ, was the host. Anyone from New York knew about Frankie. He helped usher in WBLS, the black music radio station. The beautiful Stacy Lattisaw opened the show. She moved around the stage with flair, singing hits like 'Jump to the Beat' and 'Love On A Two-Way Street.' Then, Alexander O'Neal rocked the mic. Finally, the place went dark, and the screens lit up. The hero of the 80s entered the scene with his brothers by his side. Smoke surrounded them, so any glimpse of their outfits was everything.

"Can you feel it? Can you feel it? C-A-N Y-O-U F-E-E-L I-T?" rang out across the arena.

It's hard to fathom getting a chance to see The Jackson 5 in concert. Ask anyone; they'll tell you I was Michael's biggest fan. There might be a picture of young Lamont wearing a red jacket with zippers somewhere, although I hope not. When 'The King of Pop' passed, I was a grown man in my 30's running basketball practice and my mother still had to call to check on me. She felt that Mike's death would hit me hard.

I was twelve or thirteen during this one particular summer trip to Brooklyn. One evening, we were out past dark. Anthony and I wanted to get some hoagies from a joint across the street. Now a hoagie down south is called a sub but up north it's a hoagie. Anthony's older brother, James Earl (remember the famous mouse catcher), was supposed to be watching us. My aunt and uncle were probably in bed for the night, so technically, we should've had our butts in the apartment.

Anyway, we're walking back with our hoagies in hand. Then thunder rang out, but the sky wasn't storming. That meant someone was shooting, so we did the first thing any black person would do and ran. We hit the apartment lobby and booked it up the stairs. I don't know how they got there so fast or why they came after us, but the police officers were right behind us, which is weird because officers should have been running toward the shooting. At our age we didn't know what exactly was happening, so the police scared the hell out of us. Our apartment was on the sixth floor, and they chased us all the way up there. As we hit the hallway, I found myself looking down the barrel of a .357 special. He pointed the gun directly at my head. I remember thinking, "he's about to kill me."

"Don't you fucking move," the officer said.

You hear of moments that black people have with the cops. Sometimes, they are horror stories passed down from older siblings or parents. The black community knows people of color are always the first to die in a horror film.

"I . . . I won't. I'm sorry." My hands trembled, and the bag shook as I held it up. "I only went to the store to get a hoagie," I said.

"Drop that fucking bag," the officer said.

His eyes were cold, and I could tell his glare didn't recognize the child in my voice.

The bag fell to the floor. "It's just a sandwich," I said.

My aunt and uncle's apartment door swang open. "Cuz? What's going on, Cuz?" James Earl asked. He's a street dude so his face seemed to recognize the moment.

The officer swiftly turned toward James Earl with the gun pointed at him. "You better fucking close that door," the officer yelled.

My once hero, mouse catcher slammed the door. I distinctly remember hearing click, click, click, and thinking this fool had locked the damn door, which let me know that my black ass wasn't getting in that apartment as long as the cops were in the hallway. With a foiled rescue plan from James Earl, my attention went back to the mayhem.

"What are you running for?" the officer asked. He had returned to his comfortable position of pointing the gun at my head.

With all that had happened, the question was the first from any of the officers, and boy was it confusing. Why are we running? Didn't this fool hear the gunshots? It amazes me how some people slip into a position of power.

"We're scared!" I said.

My response seemed to make the police even more confused. They blinked their eyes, looked at one another, and finally, one of them motioned to the bag. Upon checking the contents, the cop discovered the obvious.

"It's just a sandwich," the officer said. He looked at his partners and lowered his gun. "Y'all get in your apartment. You have no business being out here this time of night."

Anthony and I jumped to our feet and rushed into the apartment after James Earl unlocked the door. My heart wouldn't stop pounding. I quickly changed out of my soaked t- shirt and even checked my pants. Fear had never entered me like that, so I wasn't sure what it could do to me.

We left New York when I was five, so I didn't grow up with white people close by. The south had its share of racism, but our community was made up of blacks and Indians for the most part. That summer, I became fearful of white people and police officers. Any trust I had in those who swore to serve and protect was broken because clearly, they had zero intentions of fighting to save me. It would be years before I could trust another cop, or white person for that matter.

Racism and death didn't control the entire narrative of my middle school years, but they played a significant role. One of the parting lessons from those days came on January 28th, 1986. The maintenance man rolled in the cube-shaped television on a squeaky cart. Typically, a television in a classroom signaled a chance to catch a nap, but everyone was alert this morning. The Space Shuttle, 'Challenger' was taking off, and we would see it live. Smiles spread across our faces, and the teachers were equally as excited. One of the astronauts was New Hampshire teacher Christa McAuliffe. It took 73 seconds for all the joy to leave our eyes as we watched all seven astronauts die in the explosion. That kind of trauma sticks with you, and I knew that death was a moment away for everyone.

My father was a hardworking man who lived in silence. Not much of a big talker at home Monday through Friday. I always thought he had a Dr. Jekyll and Mr. Hyde type personality. He did what was necessary for those early years, but winding down with a few drinks was a regular occurrence, even more so during family gatherings. It's safe to say my daddy was a high-functioning alcoholic. Drinking occasionally started outside with my uncles and cousins while cooking out on the grill. Later, they transitioned to the card table, where a competitive game of spades took place. Spades were a necessary good and evil in our family. It's great to have fun, but you better not mess around and renege during spades. This was some serious shit. Family issues and arguments often started from a loss at spades.

My cousin and her husband used to swing by our house for a game of spades. When my father got a beer taste in him, he became a jokester, the guy you really didn't want to win because he would make it painful. He would run his mouth, and people gravitated toward his playful nature. I was always looking around, wondering who this guy was because he didn't converse much when he was sober. Back then, when you had somebody in trouble during spades, you licked the back of that card and stuck it to your forehead, and slammed the card on the table. Unfortunately, my cousin's husband couldn't handle losing. They would go home afterwards, and he would fight with her for not playing up to his expectations. I found this out many years later, and it gave me a different perspective on those games. I mean it was serious, but it shouldn't have been that damn serious.

My Father, Willie

Budweiser was my father's drink of choice, so I came by it naturally. Middle school is when I started dabbling with partying and drinking. Out of loneliness, I would go to my Aunt Mag's house to hang out with her and my cousins. Times were more relaxed at their house. I would spend a lot of time with a couple of guys, Chris Floyd and Lavender Ford, or affectionately known as Patches. We called ourselves cousins mainly because we were as close as family, not to mention I think everybody in that small town are kin somehow. We also worked together picking up leaves in the tobacco fields. If you lived in North Carolina and were poor, you worked those fields. It was a type of modern-day slavery if you ask me. The mas . . . I mean, the boss was a white guy, which was the case for most businesses. It was your first introduction to the American way you would be forced to accept. Work your black ass to death so you can create white family wealth.

The workday would start at 6:00 in the morning when the pickup truck started honking the horn. A group of us would jump in the back and head to the fields. Those cold and damp mornings were just plain awful. I wanted to stay in bed, but work was waiting. We started before the sun was up and took our soda and a nab (Nabisco cracker) break around 10:00 am. Everyone grabbed a Pepsi or Coke and a peanut butter nab. The decent bosses would offer a honeybun, but that was rare from those cheap ass exploiters. Savoring that cold soda didn't last long because work started again after 15 minutes. The sun was beating on you by then, and enduring it was a must until noon for lunch.

The truck would drop you off at home for one hour. Most of the guys in my group went to Aunt Mag's house for a pot of rice and beans and some crispy fried chicken if we were lucky. We did this every day during the summer. Our meals were always enjoyed in the company of Victor Newman. Yes, we took our lunch in front of the television to watch *The Young and the Restless.* Sometimes we got lucky, and the truck was ten minutes late picking us up, so we caught the beginning of *The Bold and the Beautiful.* Most times, the boss was on time at 1 p.m. to take us back to the fields. We stayed until 6 p.m. You believe that shit? How was this not illegal yet?

We were gone twelve hours a day for $20 a day. Yeah I know you're reading this saying, "Damn that's some bullshit! I would never!" Yes you would. A honeybun giving boss might pay $25, and those who felt terrible would pay $30. I never had the privilege of finding a boss who paid $30, but I discovered the $25 a day after four years on the clock. We didn't know any better. What's $100 a week to a middle schooler? It's everything. I can imagine it was more like nothing to the adult workers whose only income came from these modern day slave owners. But hey, as kids we worked for an important purpose. We wanted to hit the skating rink on Saturdays with money to spend. Our taste for the brewskis started somewhere along this timeframe. My crew and I would get tipsy before we went and ready to get a little rowdy if need be. We would go there toasted, looking for the girls and ready to lay hands on the haters from the other sections in our county.

As bad as working the tobacco fields was, picking cucumbers and blueberries were worse. I didn't understand the system and assumed a bag full of large cucumbers would get me more money since it's more cucumbers. The buyers wanted the tiny cucumbers so they could pickle them. Some of those blueberry picking jobs took me 45 minutes or more from the house to Elizabeth-town, North Carolina. Picking blueberries is an awful job and I was awful at it. The Mexicans moved to the area and got hired for the same jobs. I learned just how fast their asses could fill a bucket with blueberries. They deserved the work they received because they understood how privileged it was for them to be in our shoes. The Mexicans didn't take anything for granted. I was more than willing to let them have that crap to themselves. That little bit of money was not worth it to me. Maybe you call it lazy but I don't care, I wasn't going to do that shit any more. I knew I just wasn't cut to be picking no blueberries. But kudos to the Mexicans. Just like in many other sectors of the American Dream, the Mexicans found something they could do that others, like me, had no time, energy, or desire to do. But yet we still complain about them coming over here taking our jobs, but we fail to mention it's mostly the jobs we don't want anyway.

Aunt Mag and Aunt Adell

***

Five hours isn't a long flight, but the older I get, the muscles start to tighten up during these trips. I've been to the Bahamas plenty of times. Most people think it's a sunny destination full of beaches and drinks with the little umbrellas sticking out. Don't get me wrong, there's always a good time to be had, but tourists don't see past the resorts.

I always talk to my stateside basketball kids about the children who live in the Bahamas. My eyes opened up once I started running basketball camps in Nassau. Real Bahamians don't live life like Americans. I noticed some houses that didn't have running water. What is paradise to tourists is like a third-world country for some natives. My very first event in the Bahamas was a shocker. Kids were warming up, and then all of a sudden without warning, the lights in the gym went out for no apparent reason. I mean, there wasn't any storm outside. In fact, it was a scorching, hot sunny day. I'm freaking out because I have a strict schedule I have to adhere to (even though I made it) but the kids continue playing as if we didn't just land in the dark.

I went over to my island connect. "What's going on? What's the problem?"

"No worries man. It will be back on eventually," my connect said.

"What the hell is that?" I asked.

I learned that the city sometimes cuts off the electricity grid without warning, and there's never a timetable for when the power turns on again. We played the first few games without power for about two hours that day, and it never bothered the locals. I asked the people back at the hotel how they handled the power loss, but confusion overtook their reactions. Apparently, there's a separate electrical grid for the tourist areas. It's messed up but their lights almost never go out. Most of the kids I work with within the states don't have to worry about such things either. We are conditioned to take things for granted.

Chapter Three

THIS TEENAGER GOT IT ALL FIGURED OUT

Buy Me A Drink!

These kids always think that you can't relate to them. They would be surprised to know that my actions nearly drove my life off a cliff many times. Most of the kids who come to my camps only have to worry about basketball. I wish the younger me only had those problems in life. I had problems I didn't even know I had.

***

Working those tobacco fields put money in my pockets. I bought the necessities like school clothes and supplies, but the rest went toward having a good time. I was basically your typical teenager. I knew it all. I was lazy and I really didn't want to be bothered unless you were giving me something, or I felt like being bothered. I took after most of my family members and had some Budweisers occasionally around the age of twelve or thirteen. By the time I was fifteen, you could hardly catch me without a drink in my hand at some point during the weekend. A routine of suds and hoops lasted through most of my young adult life.

Although putting the alcohol away is a regular occurrence on my mother's side of the family, alcoholism runs deep in my father's family. My father and his brothers all dealt with the disease. I mentioned before that my father was a high- functioning alcoholic, so it rarely threatened his employment. He was one of those friendly drunks. However, his drinking did come with several consequences that he doesn't like to discuss. My father had several charges for driving under the influence during my teenage years. His license was taken away, and he got locked up a few times. The decision to drink alcohol reduced my father to riding a moped around town. It embarrasses him to talk about it these days, but that's a part of the life that he chose, at least that's what society felt back then.

Alcoholism, for many years, was not looked upon as a disease but rather just a choice. But are we considering the factors that contribute to the need to drink? Financial poverty, hereditary depression, as well as other factors, such as just trying to make it as an oppressed black man with his country fighting against, sometimes even while he was fighting for his country. I don't believe his alcoholic time period is anything to be ashamed of. In fact I do believe if he hadn't experienced those very dark and turbulent times he might not have turned out to be as great of a man as he is. So to me his story is one of inspiration for many to look up to.

It would be easy to blame the Vietnam War for my father's drinking habits, but he started indulging in the spirits before going there. That's not to say that the trauma he experienced in the Army, when a large percentage of his body was burned, didn't exacerbate his condition. My Uncle Rob was one who the war directly affected tremendously with drinking. He couldn't function, whereas my father could. Being the mischievous boys we were, I would watch my cousin Dwight sneak up behind Uncle Rob and clap his hands as loud as possible. He would scream and hold his head. We didn't understand what this was doing to him, or why he screamed. We just felt it was funny. Although I do admit I had a conscience and didn't like to look at the agony on his face. The war took away his ability to live a quality life after returning home, and our actions didn't help. It's one of those things you never forget you did as a child because as an adult I can only imagine the traumatic experience my Uncle Rob relived each time we committed such a foolish and immature act.

Unfortunately, Uncle Rob passed away due to complications of alcoholism. My grandaddy (my father's father) was also an alcoholic. His name was Nathaniel Taylor, but people called him Horsefly. I vaguely have memories with my grandfather, some were of his humor and quiet, calm demeanor when he was sober. But there are also memories I have that are not the ones you reminisce with a smile.

Uncle Rob lived with my grandparents after the war, and it wasn't always an ideal situation. I remember being fearful whenever I was visiting my grandparents house, because my granddaddy and Uncle Rob would be drinking and I knew they were not going to get along too long before it would get ugly. Sometimes they would argue and try to hurt each other with bricks and shovels. Witnessing such violence between family members was awful. I think that image of those two strong men in my family trying to kill each other scarred me. Again, I was already learning to fear death, and I believed at any minute during one of those fights one of them would die. My mother used to really worry about me because of a history of alcoholism on my father's side and a history of mental illness on her family's side. She believes that stress might trigger one of those genes. Sometimes I did feel like I was losing my mind and alcohol did stay by my side for many years but I'm thankful that neither of them took me under.

Growing up, my house was one of the places where kids played basketball. Dexter, Marlowe, Pat, Charles, Terry, and a few other cats always came by. The rules weren't too strict since we lived in the country, but my mother, along with some of the other parents in that day and age, had a few specific things I had to live by. One was I better have my ass home before that street light came on. Back then there were no cell phones with the time on it or an app to tell you what time the sun would set. No, you developed a sixth sense as to exactly how far you could push it before that street light would start to flicker on.

One day, I was with Dexter and Marlowe, skipping school. It was around 1985 or 1986. We decided to go to an old country store close to the city limits about three miles away. Dexter was old enough to drive, so we jumped in his whip. The door of the store had one of those bells that chime every time it opened and closed. This little old white lady was working the counter, and she probably noticed three young brothers up to no good. Maybe my sweating for no reason tipped her off, but she was right to be suspicious. I'm not sure who put things into motion, but we decided to snatch and run.

I had never stolen anything a day in my life, but the decision had been made. Dexter and Marlowe did their thing and moved on. My criminal inexperience kept me at a slower pace. I should've stopped as soon as I grabbed a Zero candy bar because I don't even like them damn things. In fact, I had never even eaten one up to that point nor have I ever since. With the stolen goods up my sleeve, I moved quickly towards the exit. The old lady's eyes followed me at each step.

"Hey, what do you have in there?" the old lady asked.

Somehow, the woman beat me to the door and tried to block my way. I was in too deep at this point, so I knocked her to the side. She grabbed my sleeve, but I pulled away. Dexter and Marlowe urged me to get into the car, and we sped away. My mind raced with questions about whether or not she noticed me or if the store had cameras or did I hurt this little old lady. I had always been taught to respect my elders, never steal, yet here I was doing wrong when I knew the difference between right and wrong. All I could do was go home at my usual time and act as normal as possible. My parents were always at work when I came home from school, so I felt safe, but the phone rang. Dexter was on the other end, explaining that the police came by to have a conversation with him. Apparently, my house was next on their list. I was shaking. My heartbeat uncontrollably as I contemplated what to do. Maybe I would take a bus to NY and go stay with family there? Everything, including suicide, crossed my mind, as I didn't know if I could handle the repercussions of being such a disappointment.

The police worried me but knowing my father worked at the county garage meant they all knew him. My big plan was to not answer the door when the cops came knocking. It worked! I watched them drive away, but those fools showed up a few hours later. They were smart enough to wait again until after my parents were home. I denied stealing anything because I knew the old lady didn't know what I had taken. Unfortunately, she was pressing charges for assault. My father went to have a conversation with the store owners. I learned the woman's husband said, "I wish I would've been there because I would've killed the son of a bitch." Imagine getting killed over a candy bar. My father had to stand there and not react to the violence in the man's voice towards his only son.

We went to court, but I continued to deny stealing anything. My mother, whom I had never lied to a day in my life, had my back throughout the entire process, which was comforting and heartbreaking. She knew that if I proclaimed my innocence, then I was innocent. The courts didn't believe in me with the conviction of a mother, so they found me guilty. I got slapped with community service and probation. Thankfully, the charges were sealed in my juvenile record. I never told my mother the truth because I lacked the courage. I couldn't deal with knowing the disappointment and betrayal she would feel. There was never the right time. I have walked with this burden and shame now for almost four decades, to this very day. I still could not utter the words out of my mouth so I felt obligated to release them in this book. She will see this and know that her precious son, Lamont, let her carry the badge of a fighting mother for all these years. Ma, I know it hurts, but your belief in me kept me from ever stealing anything again, possibly saving my life but if nothing else, creating my integrity. The guilt was too much. I'm sorry ma, I hope you can forgive me.

Around the same time, I wanted a dirt bike, but my mother was never down with the dangerous bikes. Don't worry, I didn't steal one, I learned my lesson. Pat and Charles, two kids from the neighborhood, had dirt bikes. I watched them zoom up and down the roads for hours. They stopped one time and offered me a ride. My mother never said I couldn't ride on one, so I accepted the offer. Pat and Charles mischievously took me on a path that led to a graveyard. The sun was starting to set, but an adventure was to be had.

We're sitting in the cemetery with the bikes turned off, why I couldn't tell you at the time because I don't know too many black folks who voluntarily hang around a cemetery.

We were only a few years past the "Thriller" video, so those images were still fresh and swimming around in my mind. Pat finally decides it's time to go, and boy was I happy. He starts his bike up, but I'm on Charles' bike, and the damn thing wouldn't start.

"Lamont, get off so I can try to get it going," Charles said.

I'm reluctant, but the need to leave the dead clouds my better judgment. Right as I step off the bike, Charles revs it up, and he and Pat speed off. They leave me with the echoes of their laughter. The night is falling, and I've been abandoned in a graveyard. Usain Bolt himself would have lost a race against me the way I hauled ass out of there. As you know, I don't have a healthy relationship with death, the dead, or any of that. I wonder if they remember that, or have any idea they contributed to my trauma enough that it had to be mentioned in my autobiography?

I had some good times in middle school, which included my first introduction to the ladies. Although I don't remember the night in question, I think I lost my virginity the summer before high school but it's possible it could have been sooner. I wish I could paint a picture of a beautiful time, but I have no clue who I slept with and exactly where it happened. It shows that either alcohol wasn't conducive to a good memory, or there were so many since then that my mind couldn't hold on to the memory. You'll soon see why and where I got my gigolo ways.

School Daze

The fall of 1986 was the start of my freshman year at South Robeson High School. I lived in Lumberton, North Carolina, with my parents, but my family and friends were in Fairmont. However, my high school was in Rowland, about a 25-minute drive from my house. Being involved in three different communities, and playing football and basketball, made me pretty popular with three various high schools. Starting off as one of the cool kids was a change in pace from how middle school had started.

Too Cool In High School

Having an excellent reputation didn't place me at the top of the food chain in my eyes. My cousin Jeff was the guy I looked up to. Sure, Dexter was an older friend I admired, but Jeff was that dude. Jeff's high school career was picturesque. He lived the life of the good-looking football and basketball star with the girlfriend who was captain of the cheerleading squad. Most times, at least when he would let me tag along, I rode shotgun around town in Jeff's car, a sky blue Cutlass Supreme with the knockin' bump in the back, so his coolness rubbed off on me. Jeff was always in mack mode with his smooth talk. My charm was developed under Jeff's tutelage. He could turn corny lines into gold standards because his confidence never broke.

"If you can get the women smiling, then you got them on the hook," Jeff said.

His advice would help me get an abundance of women for years to come. Jeff would walk up to a fine lady and say, "Would you marry me." They would smile so hard, and the conversation took off from there. To anyone else, including me at first, it's a corny ass line, but Jeff always had it cocked and loaded for delivery. You can bet I stole that line, and it worked for a single version of me many times. Learning Jeff's skills allowed me to be the best version of my worst self, but I mean that in a good way.

I witnessed and learned his craft. Jeff wrote the book on how to be a male gigolo and I was the teacher's pet. Jeff was the original "Mr. Steal Your Girl" and I wanted to be him.

Jeff was Aunt Mag's son, so I studied and learned from him for years. He always made sure I came correct. Jeff's blue Cutlass was something to envy. He kept it shining, and his system bumped the best music. We would take his ride to The Rec on Sundays. It was always packed with people, especially on Sunday, similar to a block party. I remember one time, Jeff was blasting Keith Sweat's 'In the Rain' as we rode up to The Rec. We emulated Will Smith's 'Summertime' by going two miles an hour so everyone would see us. The sun was bright, and there wasn't a cloud in the sky, but Jeff had his windshield wipers on the entire time Keith Sweat was playing. How corny is that shit? But it worked because his coolness and confidence were unmatched, and everyone was aware.

Jeff had what seemed like the whole world in his hands and scholarships for football and basketball. Timing doesn't always wait for you to do the right thing, and Jeff got this chick pregnant, losing the cheerleading girlfriend in the process. Back then, schools didn't like when your sexcapades turned you into a parent, so they pulled the scholarships. Getting a girl pregnant was a death sentence for your career. Jeff stuck around like so many others, and he took a job at one of the local plants. While I was fresh in the Navy, Jeff was around 22 or 23, when one night after completing a shift at work, he left the club and got into a car accident. He rolled his car over and ended up paralyzed from the waist down. I remember my wife at the time coming to see me on the ship, which was unusual. Her face told me something was wrong, and she could barely get it out.

The news devastated me. Jeff was and will always be my favorite cousin. Too much history with us; from the girls to the physical fights, we were like brothers. We don't talk as much as we used to, but we damn sure text each other during every Duke vs. North Carolina game. He's a true North Carolina Tarheel fan and I'm a diehard Duke fan. He used to get on me about the teams I liked back then, Duke in college and Larry Bird and the Celtics in the NBA. He would always say, you a white boy lover because all the cool hooping brothers played with Carolina, like Jordan and Worthy, and with the Lakers like Magic and Kareem.

Thanks to my acquired skillset from Jeff, I experienced my fair share of the ladies. It didn't matter who she was, when she was locked in on my radar there was a high chance she was going to become a part of my history. She could smile at me, laugh at a joke, get drunk, or smoke crack, it didn't matter, your boy was in there. But my heart was a different story, and it wasn't long before I caught my first feelings. Infatuation kicked in, and playing the part of the loyal boyfriend meant something to me. Debbie was the first chick that taught me things I didn't know about the bedroom. It makes you wonder who taught her, considering we were both in the 9th grade. Hmm . . . anyway. I was a dog in heat and a werewolf howling at the moon when it came to Debbie. I would've broken down a fence or smashed through a window to get next to her. I don't know if it was that perfectly shaped booty or that commercial worthy jeri curl, but either way I was head over heels. Like most teenagers we were smashing hips every chance we got.

We even did it in her house while her parents were home.

To make matters worse, I remember her doorway had no door but instead had those long beaded curtains hanging from the door frame, and that was it. Debbie's mom and stepdad watched TV in the living room while we were exploring teenage lust just behind a thin group of beads. My heart confused lust for love, but I was all in, I mean all the way in. My foolish ways led me to experience infidelity from a woman for the first time, albeit, not my last. The word around town was circulating that Debbie had a special friend in her little, small town called Rowland. He was this older guy from our school. She denied the allegations, but we split. Later on, I confirmed ol' dude was hitting the skins. I think my loss of trust and respect for women started there. Sure I had been with plenty of girls but they were all flings. They were meaningless to me and I was meaningless to them, just fun. But Debbie was different. At the tender age of fifteen, I could have seen myself loving her forever, with kids and a family dog. But boy, did I learn early the pain of betrayal of the heart. I just don't think I was the same after that.

I did try to do the sweetheart thing all over again in my sophomore year. Her name was Sherita, and she was the love I had waited for. She was younger, but her maturity surpassed the other females, and even mine, honestly. We met in typing class, and I knew she was the one for me from day one. We started dating in high school, and things were going well. It was like I was on the same path as Jeff. Sherita was the cheerleader, and I was a football and basketball jock. We broke up a few times, but I always carried enough charm to keep our relationship going through high school. Hey, I even introduced this one to the family. That's love. I had been burned by Debbie, so my guard was always a bit high. Once again, the rumors started swirling about my girl stepping out. This was worse than Debbie though because the person in question was my dog, my ace, my day one partner, and a football and basketball teammate. It was my boy, Willie.

I approached Willie at football practice and spoke with a broken heart and angered by betrayal. "I heard what you did, and I'm gonna beat your ass after practice." I meant it too. I was going to do my best to beat the breath out of him. Nobody crosses me like that, especially someone who is supposed to be my boy.

"I don't know what you're talking about," Willie said. "I didn't do nothing, man."

"Yeah, well, we're gonna see if I can jog your memory because I'm gonna whoop that ass," I said.

The rest of the team got excited because everyone wants to see someone get their ass beat. The coaches would give some of the players a ride home on the back of the pickup trucks in our area, so everyone was gathered around waiting. Willie was sitting on the back of one of the trucks, acting like I was just gonna let it slide. Did this guy not hear what I said to him twice?

"Hey, c'mon get down. It's time to get this ass whooping," I said. I was heated that Willie made me say it again like I wasn't about that life.

"Man, go on ahead with that. Go on now," Willie said. He waved me off like I was gonna just go away.

"Naw, get on down before I drag your ass down."

The fellas were chanting and hyping up the moment. They told Willie he was being scared. Peer pressure can get you into things where the math doesn't add up. Willie got down. The man didn't want to fight, but here we were. *Pop-pop.* And there he went. I caught the boy with a two-piece and proceeded to keep my word by beating that ass. The coaches showed up and pulled me off. To be honest, I don't remember us ever addressing the situation afterward, but to this day me and Willie are still cool. Sherita claims she and Willie never happened, but I always had my doubts. We continued dating after the incident, but she eventually ended our relationship. I don't know how our love turned sour. Sherita says I couldn't stop being a whore, and maybe she's right, but I don't quite remember it the same way. We went our separate ways, but Sherita and I remained good friends for years after. It's funny how some friendships survive chaotic moments and tumultuous relationships.

Being the player that I was, you get into unpleasant situations. I targeted women whether they had a man or not. In fact, most of the time I preferred that they had a man because then there's no chance of them wanting a serious commitment from me. I started conversing with this woman named Anne, who had a boyfriend named Evan. I guess Evan didn't like me. Whatever, who cares. A lot of cats don't like me. One night, I went with Chris and Patches to Guy Taylor Club in the country part of Fairmont. This spot was hitting, but it was deep in the woods. It was like an old schoolhouse from back in the day that was turned into a party spot. We're listening to music, checking out the ladies, and drinking. You know, the usual.

Patches looked across the way and grinned. He tapped me on my shoulder and pointed. "Hey, Lamont. Isn't that the dude Evan who has a problem with you over there?"

"Oh, yeah, that's him," I said.

"Well, are you ready to handle this?" Patches asked. "Let's do it."

That's how we rolled. We walked over, and I looked him in the eye.

"Yo, what up?" I asked.

"What's . . ?" Evan asked.

This cat had the audacity to respond to my question. Before I knew it, I just reacted out of instinct and punched Evan dead in his mouth before he finished speaking. I'm beating his ass, and then Gene, his cousin, pulled me off and said, "Hell no, that ain't how it's going down." Everyone knew Gene. He was this big ass muscular boxer and had a reputation for knocking cats out.

Well, Chris' brother, Frog, was there. He's what we called cock-strong. Frog was the star football running back who never lifted weights but could push over a car. He stood 6'3 and had rusty hardworking knuckles. His only drawback though was his hard stutter. Frog got in the middle of things and said, "W- W-W-W-Wait one damn minute now. Ain-Ain-Ain't gonna be n-n-no jumpin'. W-W-W-We doing this one on one."

Everyone went outside so we could bang in the parking area. Well, Evan's punk-ass went running. I knew he didn't want to bang, but I thought he would take his beating like a man. This fool ran and got a rifle and pointed it directly at me. He chased me around, and I knew he would shoot if I stopped running. Evan came from a sketchy environment (fast forward, Evan did eight years in prison). While dodging around cars, I toss my keys to Patches. He pops my trunk and gets one of the guns for me. I can't tell you exactly why or where we got guns from, but we rode around with them for times like this. Evan and I start shooting, but after a few shots, everyone hauls ass.

We didn't go at it after that night. I'm still cool with Anne. It's funny we never tried to move past friendly conversations. My popularity with the ladies had people assuming a conversation with me would always lead to something. I don't blame them. I was probably a real threat.

The ladies had influenced me quite a bit. At 16, hormones introduced me to my first entanglement with a grown woman. I met her at a club called The Country Kitchen. That was my favorite spot. It was a country spot just over the state line into South Carolina and they didn't card the young brothers who didn't want violence, just drinks and a chance to pull a tenderoni. I was there with my usual partners doing our everyday thing when Marvin Gaye's 'Let's Get it On' was spinning. For some reason I couldn't stop watching this one couple on the dance floor. This 20 something year-old redbone swayed to the music, and she hypnotized me. Her name was Brownie, and the guy was her husband. She acted as if that was her favorite song, so I was determined to make it our song. As soon as her husband went to get in a game of pool, I slipped $5 to the DJ to replay our song. I asked Brownie to dance, and we hit the floor. She was a grown woman, and her body, her smell, and her movements did it for me. Up until that point I had never entertained an older woman. We exchanged numbers.

Our relationship quickly turned sexual. I would pick Brownie up down the street from her house, and we had some wild times. We carried on after I turned 17, and I enjoyed feeling grown. I picked Brownie up one day, and her mood was different.

"Lamont, I'm pregnant," Brownie said.

Seemingly unbothered I said, "Cool. What are you and your husband going to name it."

She huffed. "What are you talking about? I told you I don't even sleep with him like that."

"That ain't my baby. I can't do this. I'm supposed to go to the military," I said.

The only thing on my mind was my cousin Jeff. I remember how his future was taken from him because he got his girlfriend pregnant. I knew it was my fault, and I understood how to prevent something like that, but at 17, I was acting like a 17-year-old who only thought he was grown.

She looked puzzled. "Take me back to the house."

Brownie never spoke to me again after that day. Years later, I briefly saw her with her husband and daughter at Walmart. My best friend Quincy was with me, and I pointed Brownie out to him. Quincy said the little girl looked like me, but that's what people always say in life. By this time Brownie was a preacher. Who was I to disrupt her family's life if I didn't need to. I know that they are happy together. What would I accomplish by destroying their household peace by even bringing up an affair she had?

My high school days of sexual conquests continued. I found another grown woman to have fun with, and she turned me out. The curvaceous beauty was 27, and she enjoyed her drinks. We always did our business at her house, and I knew she had a man. I got out of school early one day and stopped by her crib, which wasn't far from my school and blew the horn repeatedly. Her toddler son opened the door.

"Is your mama home?"

The boy ran inside and returned. "Yes." "Can you tell her to come outside?"

He ran inside again. "She said to come inside."

I'm not thinking anything of the situation except hope she's in the mood. I stroll in, and the door closes behind me. I turn to see Roger, one of the biggest niggas I had ever seen in my life.

"Helen, get your ass out here. Somebody is here to see you!" Roger yelled. He had that Deebo look in his eyes. You know, crazy yet scary.

I'm thinking, oh, shit. I was a big guy for a high school football player, but this nigga looked about 30 and was drooling like he wanted a snack. He had me scared as hell. Helen came out and did her best acting job.

"Is this what the fuck you wanted?" Roger asked. "What are you talking about?" Helen asked.

"This is what you wanted, right?" Roger never takes his eyes off of me. "Look, bruh. I'm gonna let you leave, but if I ever catch your mutherfucking ass at my house again, it's not going to end well for you."

I was justified in my silence, but in my head, I was saying, yes, sir. Roger opened the door and let me leave. That was another one of my close calls when it came to being with somebody else's woman.

In-between sexual activities with various women, I managed to get my first real job at Hardee's. That same week, I got my first real car. She was a clean two-door red Ford Mustang. I would go around to the Pool Hall in Rowland after work, to where the fellas were lounging. My trunk was always packed with hamburgers and fries. The restaurant always had abundant leftovers, and I was tasked to throw them away at the night's end. I always ensured the food ended up in my car instead of the dumpster. The guys were hungry, probably from smoking weed all evening, so they couldn't wait to see my car pull up.

Hardee's was a decent gig, but the longest job I had was the one Mom got for me at Shoney's. She served in the restaurant, so she was able to put a good word in for me, which I was thankful for. Right after leaving Hardee's, I worked in a Chinese joint, but I had to escape. They tried to work the dog out of me in the nastiest environment I had ever seen in my life. My mother doesn't like for me to mention what I saw because she still eats their food. I was out after one day on the clock. The move to Shoney's saved my teenage work life. Mom worked during the day, and I washed dishes at night, so our interaction was minimal. Keep in mind that drinking alcohol had been part of my life for a few years, so I was getting tipsy on the side. Mom never knew, and I wanted to keep it that way.

One night, I chilled in the back parking lot with a white and   a black coworker. We were getting faded with the sauce. The white guy said we should go back into the restaurant, which was closed at the time. We all knew the side door didn't lock, and the alarm system didn't work. Why not go in and treat ourselves. Looking back it never occurred to me that the white guy could make the decision to go in so easily because his repercussions would be much less. We proceeded to cook an entire meal as if the restaurant was open. The black coworker decided to take things a little too far by stealing the television management used for training videos. He took the set to an abandoned house with no roof. We thought it was funny, then it started raining. You guessed it, the TV was destroyed. Management never found out who stole the television. That's one of the many things that happened to me because I chose alcohol over common sense.

Another unforgettable moment from my time at Shoney's involved Jeff, one of the cooks. He was another of those cock- strong brothers who was blessed with muscles without working for them. Now I'm just doing my work and I can't wait to get off of work so I can join the fellas for some fun. Jeff crosses my path.

"Lamont, I'm gonna beat your ass after work," Jeff said. What the hell did I do to Jeff ? I didn't want those problems, but I wasn't going to act like no punk either. "You ain't about to do nothing," I said. To be clear, I didn't want that smoke from Jeff. The guy was kind of scary. Everyone started leaving after work, but I hadn't heard a peep from Jeff the rest of the night. Maybe he was talking just to talk. There were four of us outside, and Jeff was one of us.

"I told you I was gonna beat your ass after work," Jeff said. Any hope for a good night dissipated. "Man, for what? What's your problem?" I asked.

"I just don't like you," Jeff said.

He doesn't like me? Since when is that a reason . . . POW! It was night time, but a blinding light suddenly appeared. This asshole punched me in my damn eye. I got brave and pretended it was about to go down. However, the first punch was enough to tell me the follow-ups would be just as impactful. Instead of swinging on Jeff, I told him I was gonna catch up with him and handle this so I jumped into my car and looked for some help. My buddy Shay came right on time. Shay might've been the most brutal dude in 10 states. He came down south from New York and brought the heart of the boroughs with him. Shay whooped many asses in the short period of time he had been down south. The brother could teach a master class on ass whooping.

"Yo, Shay!" I yelled.

"What's up, Mont?"

We all know one punch had me questioning the meaning of life, but what came out my mouth was, "They jumped me, man." I told a tale of Jeff and his buddies trying me. Shay wasn't about to let his boy get got like that.

"Hell Nah." Shay and his friend jumped in my car. We headed to Hardee's, where Jeff and his cronies would be, so I could gain back the respect I lost. "Let's go, Lamont. We gonna go handle this shit right now," Shay said.

I'm thinking, finally, someone will knock Jeff out. My confidence was blazing because I had the baddest backup around.

"Yo, Jeff, what's that bullshit you were talking?" I asked. "You thought you were just gonna jump me?" I could've won an Oscar with my performance.

"I ain't jump you. I punched you in the eye myself," Jeff said.

"Oh, y'all gonna jump, my man. We're gonna handle this outside right now," Shay said.

My plan was working to perfection. We would squabble outside, and Shay would handle Jeff while I tangled with someone less threatening. Watch Shay dust these dudes off. Jeff's crew was about to witness North Carolina's version of Mike Tyson.

Shay bounced back and forth. His fists were ready for action. "Alright, nobody's jumping in. It's straight up. Lamont vs. Jeff."

Ummm wait, say what? Shay went off-script at the most inopportune time. This was supposed to be their rumble, the Shay and Jeff show. I ran from an ass-whooping only to end up in the same predicament. We squared up, and Jeff snatched me up. A grizzly bear would've been impressed by how hard this nigga was squeezing the life out of me. The only thing to do was hit him upside the head with both fists. My punches went unnoticed by Jeff, who wasn't releasing his death grip. I never imagined finding so much happiness at the sight of the police. Lumberton P.D. pulled up right before the last breath left my body.

We all dispersed, and to my surprise, the fight is considered a classic draw. Some people thought I won because I delivered a 50-hit combo to the dude's head, but I know Jeff didn't feel that. Giving me the victory was like declaring Sugar Ray Leonard the victor in his second fight with Tommy Hearns. I knew there was less than 30 seconds of air left in me before the cops showed up. We never had a conversation about that fight. Jeff grew up to be a good guy, and we are Facebook friends. I need to ask him, "Why in the hell did you want to fight me anyway?" Life was crazy back then. He might not even remember, I'm sure he beat many asses for no reason.

I was all about the ladies in high school, but the fighting and drinking messed up my schooling during my 11th-grade year. I was taking skip days because I had my car. My parents assumed everything was going well because I never brought my foolishness around the house. I had a teacher named Ms. Peterken who taught Algebra

II. A lot of students didn't like her because she held you accountable and wasn't about that bullshit. Showing up five minutes late might get you kicked out of her class for the day. I failed Algebra II, and I didn't care. My future was set without passing her class. However, I received a 37% in Ms. Peterken's class, and deep inside, I knew I was better than that grade. She knew it too and dug in.

I had a meeting with the guidance counselor to schedule classes for senior year. She mentioned Algebra II. I said, "Nah, I already took it, and I don't want to retake it." Right on cue, in walked Ms. Peterken.

"Oh, no, you're taking that class again. You gave me no effort, and I know what you're capable of," Ms. Peterken said. She turned to walk out. "I'll see you in the fall."

She spent the year treating me like her teacher's pet. She called me out to answer questions, and the class laughed because they knew I had taken her class before. I applied myself for the entire year and worked my way to 91% in Ms. Peterken's class. Not only did I grasp the concepts, but I realized I was good at math. Years later, I had to take Algebra when I went back to college. I excelled in each math course and always finished second in the class, the Chinese dude in my class made it clear none of us were on his level. My instructor even suggested changing my major to math. Hell no I thought, I hate math and school.

Later I would realize it was the competitive drive in me that pushed me to excellence.

Outside of the 37%, my grades were always respectable in high school without much effort. I was having too much fun to fully apply myself. Most kids go to their junior and senior prom, but I attended three proms. The first was during my freshman year when I dated a senior. Mom didn't like that her baby was dating an older woman, but she had no idea how older the females got after 9th grade. She was right to have mixed feelings about my first prom date because, boy, Peggy was good to me. Junior year was Reeva, and it was cool, we were just really good friends. I decided to go stag for my senior year. I wore a polka-dot outfit reminiscent of Kwame and a low-brimmed hat mirroring Whodini. I had the freshest attire at the dance. You couldn't tell me anything. Being myself was always more important than falling in line with the trends.

1990 Senior Year High School Prom

My school daze was primarily because of my party style. We fought a lot, and I don't know why. Perhaps the drinking mixed with testosterone amped us up. Who knows. One night I was kicking it with Patches and Chris at Aunt Mag's house. She was at work, and cousin Jeff was with his homeboys. It was a night of drinking Budweiser and Mad Dog 2020, the cheap liquor drink made for alcoholics and broke teenagers who want to get drunk cheap and blank out from alcohol poisoning. For future reference, heavy beer and banana red or grape don't mix well in the stomach. The sounds of a country night and hip-hop on the stereo set the scene for some teenage fun, but I don't know what happened next. I broke through the fog from hearing my name and Jeff standing over me. I woke up in the bathtub fully clothed, but I was drunk as shit.

"Lamont! Lamont! What the fuck is this?" Jeff asked. He pulled me into the living room.

The smell hit me in the face and stirred the pot of poison in my stomach. I couldn't believe what I saw. There was a massive pile of human shit on the coffee table. Jeff could've ended my life by how angry he was.

"You have to be a nasty muthafucka to pull down your pants and shit on the coffee table," Jeff said. "Who did it, Lamont?"

I wished I could blame Patches or Chris, but neither of us knew who delivered the steamy substance. It was all summed up by a night of drunken stupidity. Ms. Bertha Mae, Chris' grandma, said, "beer and watermelon don't mix." Well, she was right because we did eat watermelon that night. I never threw up so much in my life.

I ended my senior year by driving to New York with the fellas. We went to a club where Big Daddy Kane would hang out. Of course, alcohol was part of the trip, and the guys spent the night smoking weed. Again, smoking just wasn't my thing. We thought there was enough money to get back to North Carolina on the ride back. Teenagers never think about the costs of tolls or important things like that. We collectively decided to skip the toll, and the police thought it was a bad idea. One of my friends had half of a weed roach in the ashtray, so the cops towed the car and took us to jail. I couldn't call Willie and Irene for help because I enjoyed breathing. They interrogated us for a few hours, mostly to scare us enough that hopefully we wouldn't do it again. The cops finally let us go, but my car was on lockdown.

An older black gentleman took us in his taxi to the impound lot. He knew the police did us dirty, and he wanted to show that the world wasn't all bad. He paid for Marlowe's car to get out the impound and gave us $50 to make it home. We took the wisdom he imparted to us and filled the tank with gas. Then, we ate like kings at a burger spot. How could we keep making mistakes? The gas light came on halfway through Virginia. Back then, people could pump gas and pay after. We did a quick pump-and-go and prayed all the way home. The lesson learned was teenagers don't know as much as they think they know. My in-the-moment thinking got me into more situations than I wanted. But high school was ending and it was time to make some adult decisions.

I turned down a few football scholarships to several Historically Black Colleges and Universities (HBCUs) because I had torn my anterior cruciate ligament and didn't want to take a chance on re-injuring myself and losing my scholarship. But then I met with Tony Gerald, a Navy recruiter, and he convinced me to start fresh somewhere away from home.

Chapter Four

FROM STUPID TEENAGER TO MILITARY MAN

Anchors Away My Boy!

All eyes were locked in, and it was apparent as to why. Every kid that participates in GetMeRecruited events usually has three personal goals. They want to showcase their skills against the best competition, earn a high ranking, and eventually get recruited by colleges. I'm not in the business of gaslighting my players, but I understand what's in their hearts, and not reaching a division one school sometimes breaks them down.

"It's a sad truth, but most of y'all aren't going to play division one basketball," I said.

Silence never sounded so loud. The kids looked at each other, wondering who I might've been talking about. Each one hoped that I didn't mean them.

"It doesn't mean that you're not good. Hell, you have to be good to have received an invitation to this camp. Sometimes, life decides to pull you in a different direction."

Amber, a junior I have known since seventh grade, raised her hand. She was solid and full of fundamentals. Amber's knowledge of the game was unmatched at her age, but the other girls had more talent and wow factors. She went to a small high school in Idaho, and her parents weren't going to move to another area because basketball might be better. Playing against weak competition has not been of benefit to her and her development.

"Go ahead, Amber," I said.

"I know my best shot at playing college ball is at a division two school, but what if I don't want that?"

"Your grades are stellar. You can easily get an academic scholarship and hope to be a walk-on. Those are the type of things I want you to ask when you are in the workshop". It was important to me that every GetMeRecruited event has educational material incorporated to help parents and players, as well as coaches, gain knowledge of the entire recruiting process. That means learning the important stuff, off the court.

"But I don't know what I would do in school, and I don't want to stay in Idaho either," Amber said.

"I see…"

I had some decisions to make when high school neared its end. I wasn't going to hang my hat on college football, but I knew academics wasn't the route I wanted to take at that time. The military isn't a bad option, and it can lead to a successful path if used correctly. It's good to have a plan B when plan A looks bleak.

***

Anthony "Tony" Gerald was the local Navy recruiter in Lumberton. Tony would pop up occasionally for events at the school, or we would see him at the mall. He would spit that military game to anyone willing to listen. A group of my friends and I seriously considered the military as an option. I knew the Army and Marines were a hard no, because I wasn't feeling that hardcore, rifle carrying in the woods, combat life. Unfortunately, I wasn't slim enough for the no huskies allowed Airforce, which was considered the easiest branch. Tony said the Navy was laidback, and they didn't mind taking on kids with some puffiness. I was sold, and so were the others. So some of my best high school friends joined the Navy.

I headed to boot camp in Great Lakes, Illinois July 2nd, 1990 and yes I was terrified. In North Carolina, I was a big fish in a small pond. Flying into O'hare airport in Chicago was intimidating to a country boy like myself. I had only known about Chicago from my favorite television show, 'Good Times'. They loaded all of us recruits into a USO van headed for Great Lakes Training Center, the largest Naval boot camp base in the country. There was an older black gentleman driving the van who convinced us not to worry because boot camp was a mind game, and we would be fine if we remembered that. By the time we were near the end of our hour-long ride we were all pretty confident that boot camp would be a breeze. Whatever restored confidence I had during the drive was erased when my CC (Company Commander), Tony, slammed the van door open.

"You get your goddamn ass out of this van right now," CC Tony said, with the face of a rattlesnake looking for an ass to bite.

I thought to myself, "Ah man I done fucked up", because I believed the violence in CC Tony's voice.

"I own you. Your parents don't exist. I'm your mama and your daddy now!"

I learned how to say, "Yes, Company Commander," with quickness. The first night was hell. They yelled, had us fill out paperwork, yelled some more, shaved our heads, and yelled some more. At 1:30 am, they said we have thirty minutes to shit, shave, and shower. Lights were out at 2 a.m. I started thinking about how that old driver bullshitted us on the way here. This wasn't a mind game. This was for real. Life sucks right now and little did I know it was only going to get worse. At 4 a.m. the bullshit started up all over again.

Bang-Bang-Bang.

Someone busted through the door with a trash can.

"Get up! Get yo asses up!"

I will never forget that moment because I had the worst headache I had ever had after being tormented all night. Welcome to boot camp.

My time in the Great Lakes wasn't too bad after making some adjustments. Each day started earlier than we wanted, and believe it or not we woke up to MC Hammer blasting in our ears every damn morning Ugh! All because CC Tony was boys with Hammer when he was in the Navy before hitting it big. Our other Company Commander was Petty Officer Byrd. He was bumped down from the Chief's ranking because of his alcoholism. The demotion didn't work because his eyes were bloodshot every day, and his breath smelled like liquor.

I was always shy when it came to crowds and learned that humiliation was my enemy. We were new, so we were being taught how to march first. CC Tony once told me to get to the front of the line to show everyone how to march. I knew this was a bad idea. I was too nervous because all the attention was on me. We got in line with me as the leader. We barely got started good when . . .

"Whoa! Whoa! Get your ass to the back of the line. You're worse than they are," CC Tony said.

I felt like I couldn't do anything right. My confidence took a hit every time the commanders called me out. One of the worst and actually best times in boot camp was when we had to stencil our names and last four digits of our social security numbers on our uniforms the next day.

"I'm only going to say this once, so pay attention. I know one of you muthafuckas will be hardheaded," CC Byrd said. "Every company has somebody hard headed as hell. Pay attention to detail!"

Those words terrified me because I didn't want to be that guy. CC Byrd did a quick run-through with the stencil board and gave us one minute to finish. I decided the board would slow me down, so I did the stencil without it and finished in only 40 seconds. As CC Byrd walked around inspecting everyone's work giving them the passing nod, he froze when he saw my shirt.

"I told you one of you stupid muthafuckas was not going to listen. Everybody, look at this dumb ass."

Not using the board caused the last four of my social skills to bleed through onto the back of my shirt. All eyes were on me.

"Your dumb ass is going to wear this shit too!" CC Bird said.

I wore that shirt for the remainder of boot camp, and because I was broke, I also wore it to my first duty station. People were always asking why in the hell my social is located on my back. My failure to pay attention to detail caused months of embarrassment. I constantly teach my players and staff the importance of attention to detail. I believe this incident turned out to be the single most contributing factor to my overall success. Over thirty years later I still remember why attention to detail is so important.

Anchors Away My Boy!

I went back home after graduating from boot camp, and enjoyed every minute of it. I felt a sense of pride and accomplishment. I remember wanting to wear my uniform around town just so people would stare or make a comment. Back then, a service uniform meant something you could really be proud of, that you were making something out of your life. But I soon returned to Great Lakes for 'A' School, where I earned my rating of Gunner's Mate Missile (GMM). Sailors didn't have much to do in their spare time, so true to their long-standing reputation, we drank a lot, and I mean a lot. My roommates consisted of Banner Demers, a 6'3 Ronald McDonald-looking white boy from Montana who turned out to be my best Navy buddy and a lifelong friend to this day. Then there was Gary Guiterrez, a cool Mexican cat from Colorado that got blackout drunk regularly. Finally there was Cameron Stout, a white kid from Indiana who was our by-the- book military roommate. He shined his shoes daily and didn't bother us much, mainly because we probably were fools and misfits in his eyes.

This was my first time being around any other races outside of mine and Lumbee Indian but it worked out. I educated them about the urban lifestyle, and they explained moose hunting and weird shit like that to me. I also learned to appreciate rock n' roll with groups like the Red Hot Chili Peppers and Journey. Go figure.

I remember we all decided we were going to chip in on a television for the room. I was too excited.

"I can't wait to watch some B.E.T.!" I said super excitingly. Banner replied, "What is that?"

I was appalled. How in the hell in 1991 could anyone not have heard of B.E.T.? I thought for sure everyone knew about that channel.

"Black Entertainment Television duh" I said.

"Bahahahahaha! Yeah right there's no such thing as black tv!" Banner said while laughing.

Well as soon as we got that television hooked up I immediately turned to B.E.T.

"See, dumbass?" I said.

"Well I'll be damned, I don't believe it." Banner mumbled in disbelief.

That was an eye opener for me, and it stuck with me. We all have different experiences in life which can lead to different perspectives. Many times it's a lack of knowledge and understanding, not necessarily an indication of hate and bigotry.

We loved to party and one of our shipmates told us about a party at his cousin's house, another Navy guy named Daniel. Because none of them had a ride, me, Banner, and Gary hitched a ride over to Dan's place. As soon as we walked in I spotted what was to me the most beautiful white woman I had ever seen. Mind you I had never been around white women, or men for that matter, much in my life anyway, so it really never crossed my mind as I would ever date one.

"Yo who is that?" I asked with gleaming eyes.

"Brittany. She's Daniels' wife," Gary said.

I was still young, so I guess you could say my frontal lobe wasn't fully developed because I didn't care whose wife she was, I wanted her. This mentality probably helps explain why I kept getting into relationships with the wrong people. Hearing that this pretty little snow bunny was Daniels' wife should've stopped me from pursuing her, but the girl was bad. Sometime during the night I was able to weasel my way into a conversation with her alone, in one of the back rooms. This led to her pouring her feelings out about her relationship. She talked about how Daniel would fight with her, mistreat her, and isolate her from the world. She was a formal model from Cali and knew no one in Illinois so Daniel would keep her locked up in the house while he hung out and drank with friends and other women. After about an hour or so of deep conversation and me showing concern while comforting her, we discussed me coming to visit her, and my time on duty made it possible. The base was divided into red, blue, yellow, and green duties. So if it was a red day, everyone who was under red had to stay on base overnight to hold down the base and complete work duties. Daniel's color was yellow, and unfortunately for him my duty fell on blue, which meant our duty times differed. So when he was stuck on base, I was free to wander.

I had one major problem though. I had no car. I asked one of my boys, Seaman Phillips, if I could use his car and he was cool with it. But that brought to light my second major problem, it was a stick shift and I had no idea how to drive a stick. But when Phillips said, "You can drive a stick can't you?"

"What kind of question is that? Of course I can drive a stick!"

Now although I had no idea how to drive a stick and there was no YouTube or even internet at that time to reference, there was nothing that existed on this earth that was going to prevent me from getting to that goddess. I was going to learn, that day. And I did, at the expense of Phillips Toyota Sentry's clutch, because it caught hell coming down Sheridan Road.

I made my first appearance at Brittany's house and our first encounter was one of a soap opera, with very little words until we were in each other's arms in a passionate session of lovemaking. This went on over several months. I was so comfortable being at their house that I would bring Gary and Banner over to hang out and drink beer while Brittany and I handled our business. Well, one afternoon while the fellas were in the living room awaiting my arrival from the bedroom, Brittany climbed on top of me. Suddenly, the door opens, and I see the silhouette of a white hat and peacoat. I instantly knew who it was! The light turns on, and anger is painted across a shocked Daniel's face.

Brittany's naked and jumps off of me. "Daniel, what are you doing at home?"

"What am I doing at home? What are you doing on top of this dude?"

I froze. Daniel had a solid build, and he knew me. I wasn't sure if I would have to fight this dude naked or not so I just laid there partly contemplating my next move and partly terrified of what was about to happen.

"Taylor, put your clothes on," Daniel said.

I listened to the man. Daniel walked into the kitchen as Brittany ran to the bathroom to cry. Instead of leaving like a rational non-alcoholic, I went into the kitchen where Daniel was to grab my beer from the fridge. I chose alcohol instead of avoiding a potential ass whooping or worse. However, Daniel wasn't in the mood to tussle. I could see the anger was not apparent but the hurt was. He asked about my relationship with his wife, and I expressed that the encounter was a one- time thing, knowing that it had actually been many times but hoping to keep what little bit of heart he had left together. Daniel said it would've been someone else if it wasn't me. They had two little girls together, so he said his plan was to just take them and leave. I apologized and tried to convince him of my sorrow and how this was a mistake and wasn't supposed to happen.

I went to class the following day, like the night before didn't matter. A fellow sailor asked if I had heard what happened. "Daniel is locked up for beating up Brittany," He said.

Phillips let me use his car again so I rushed over right after class. It took some convincing to get Brittany to come downstairs because she didn't want me to see her in that condition. I saw just how bad Daniel beat her up. Two black eyes, a broken rib, and a host of body bruises. Thankfully, Brittany left him and went to a shelter with the girls. She would come to the barracks and visit me from time to time with the kids in tow but eventually she got a place in Vernon Hills, Illinois and worked on herself. We even started dating.

Surprisingly, Brittany taught me a lot about music, like Parliament with George Clinton and Rick James. I didn't know a white girl could be so cool. I mean she wasn't one of those white girls that "act black." She was just naturally cool. From that point on I just thought Cali had to be the mecca of cool ass white girls and movie stars. She was once the babysitter for B2K and that clique. In fact, one of her best friends back in Cali was Monyee, the twife at the time of producer Chris Stokes. She would often talk about little Omarion and Marques Houston. We kicked it for quite awhile. I would babysit for her while she worked on getting her nursing degree. I always felt guilty about breaking up Brittany's family, but she assured me that things worked out for the best.

I was able to track her down on a visit to the area many years after that. She was right, it seemed as if things had really worked in her favor. Her girls were all grown up, one driving a Benz while finishing up high school and the other one driving a BMW in college. Brittany was, by then, one of the leading nurses of a big hospital in downtown Chicago. And it must've paid well because she stayed in this huge house by a lake on a golf course. I was happy and relieved that things were good for her. I mean Brittany was my first affair with a married woman in the military, but unfortunately she wouldn't be my last. And you know how the saying goes, what goes around comes around.

US Navy Roommates And I Drinking In North Chicago

At that time me and the fellas loved to play basketball and the gym on base was the spot. There was this chick that all the fellas sweated named Kathy. She was a sexy mid-20 something brown skinned honey who had a fit body and man she could hoop. That was such a turn on. She was the bomb in a sweatshirt and jogging pants and could hit a jumper like Jordan in game 6. For the most part Kathy was like one of the guys, but there was no denying her sex appeal. Only one problem, Kathy was married to a Marine recruiter. That stopped most of the cats from even trying her. Not me. I mean I didn't just set out to conquer Kat but she would be flirtatious. We became cool, real cool. I didn't have a car and Kathy had a hoopty ride with no heat in it. Well one day after hooping, Kathy and I decided to go to the bowling alley on base. I had no car so we had to go in hers and there was three feet of snow on the ground. It was about 10 degrees. That didn't matter because in the parking lot of that bowling alley it was 110 degrees! We had an affair that night and Kathy was hooked on the young boy.

Over the course of the following few weeks Kathy would invite me to her crib to meet her husband, and even though she said he knew about me being her cool hooping partner, I wasn't feeling it. However, she finally convinced me to come for dinner, I mean all her details of her skills in the kitchen were appealing to ya boy's eating habits. She knew what she was doing.

They lived near downtown Chicago. Her husband was a Marine recruiter for the area and was actually a pretty cool cat. He worked on Harrier helicopters and loved showing me the dynamics of his job. We ate a great delicious dinner that Kathy cooked while we sat in the living room and talked about the military. We drank beer, laughed, and one would've thought we were the best of buds. As the night got later and we were both pretty toasted, I was expecting Kathy's husband to give me a handshake and tell me to be careful as I hit the road back to Great Lakes, I mean that's what the hell I would've done. Instead they both agreed to get me a blanket and pillow for the couch for the night. Early that morning I was awakened by Kathy whipping up breakfast but I continued to play the sleep role. I watched as hubby got dressed in his Marine's finest uniform and gave her a kiss on the cheek and walked out the door. I must've dozed back off to sleep because I only remember being reawakened by Kathy's kiss, telling me it's time to eat. I get up, eat an amazing breakfast, and proceed to make love to Kathy on the living room floor, literally less than an hour from watching her receive a loving kiss from hubby. This taught me some early valuable lessons. One, no nigga stays the night and two, if he must stay, then when my ass leaves, he leaves.

A few months later, as Kathy and I had become regular lovers, I could tell she was becoming more emotionally invested in our connection. She would come to the gym on base more often, acting more girlfriend-ish, and even attempting to flirt with others to make me jealous. It did work occasionally, not because I cared for her as a girlfriend, I think it's just natural for a man to not want another man to touch what he has. I mean I liked her and all but that was only for my enjoyment. Even her husband was privileged to have time with her in my mind. Anyway, I went to visit Kathy one night while hubby was away and she met me outside, tears in her eyes.

"What's wrong with you?" I said.

"I'm pregnant." She replied.

"Y'all didn't want any more kids?" I curiously asked with all seriousness.

"Huh? Are you serious? It's like that?" now with anger in her voice.

I was confused. Surely she wasn't insinuating this baby was mine. I mean what do I look like, boo boo the fool.

"Fuck you! Don't worry about it!" she yelled as she walked in her apartment and slammed the door.

I never heard from Kathy again. She never even came back to the gym on base. At least, not that I'm aware of.

Around this time I was training in Gunner's Mate A School and making money, so I splurged and bought my first car, a brand spanking new red 1990 Dodge Shadow. The first day after leaving the dealership I went straight to the auto custom shop and got my baby tricked out. I had the boomin' system, tinted windows, and the latest high tech cellular phone mounted on the inside. You couldn't tell me nothing! One nice day while cruising through the hood bumping Too Short and NWA, I spotted a fly slim redbone walking by named Tasha. I laid on the country boy charm and of course I got the digits.

Once I got back to the barracks and all the fellas were sitting around bullshittin', I was telling them the story of how I met ol' girl. My man Walt said he got lucky and met one today too. I said but mine is this pretty slim redbone. Walt said his girl was too. Turns out my man Walt had met the same girl and received a number too. Damn, what the hell? And I was feeling her too. But what we discovered is Tasha gave us two separate numbers, so we decided whoever had the right number would be the one who got the other one's blessing. Well, my number was valid thus why I can continue telling the story.

Tasha and I started dating, and we usually hung out at her sister Nee Nee's house in the projects in North Chicago. My knowledge of the hood was for the most part people left you alone if you minded your own business. I mean everybody knew I was Tasha's boyfriend, the Navy boy, who would be outside drinking and playing music not bothering anyone. So one day, as every other day, I was just sitting in my car in front of the apartment drinking beer and minding my damn business. Tasha got on my nerves about something silly, which sparked an argument. Me being the hothead I was at the time, I jumped in my whip and went speeding around her complex, only to crash into the back of another car. With my front end smashed up, I circled back to Nee Nee crib, yelling for Tasha to come outside.

About this time, up came some visitors that had seen the crash. You see there's this huge family in the hood with a pair of twins, Darnell and Mike, whose last names were, ironically, Hood, and they were known for mixing it up. It was snowing and my car was smashed so I wasn't up for no bullshit, not to mention I really had a quick temper back then. Darnell walked by, making a smart-ass remark, so I said something slick back. So

Mike decided to chime in. I guess they woke up and chose violence. But I guess they didn't realize I was about that life.

A fight ensued and before you know it, while I'm punching one brother, the other is choking me from behind. Their sister, Vicki, started kicking the shit out of me. Out of nowhere my future sister-in-law Nee Nee decided to make it a family affair, so she jumped on Vicki's ass and started giving her the business. It was a ghetto battle royale in the snow. Tasha, who they wouldn't let come outside because we thought she was pregnant, opened the door and released her mother, Dot. Now Dot didn't play no games, and she came out with the .357 and let a few rounds off in the air. The police showed up and locked up the Hood family, Nee Nee, Tasha, and my ass.

Of course when you're in a drunken state, you think you're smarter than you really are, so when we got to the police station I told the arresting officer I was the legal age of 21 and hid my ID under papers on his desk. They booked me and sat me in a cell by myself. I was in there drenched in blood and melted snow and vomited for what seemed like hours. Eventually we were released to the custody of Tasha's grandpa. No matter how drunk I was, I can't forget riding home in his station wagon with a dozen of the street cats he nurtured crawling all over us.

I returned to the base with a case pending. It was later dropped in exchange for the assault charges against the brothers being dropped. Basically a wash. Just some ignorant asses fighting. One thing I can say for sure though, the hood respected me for simultaneously taking on two of its giants from that day on.

I did well in A School, and the way we received our next duty station was that the students with the best grades got the best picks. So I had a decent pick and I chose my ship, the USS Mahan stationed in Charleston, SC for my first duty station. Only one problem though, the USS Mahan was in the Persian Gulf and they had just started a 6 month cruise. I was ordered to meet them in Bahrain, Saudi Arabia. But my relationship with Tasha was going well, so of course I didn't want to leave her behind. I mentioned to my mother that I wanted Tasha to stay with her while I went off to the Gulf. You know Irene, she wasn't having me shacking up with someone.

"Y'all must be getting married." Mom said. "I bought a ring," I said.

"You might as well get married as soon as you get here."

So, sure enough we got married in a small wedding in Dillon, South Carolina, days later. Tasha was in her best off- white outfit and I was in my Navy Blues. But with the help of divine intervention I was informed that my ship, the U.S.S. Mayhan was full and I would have to wait for a bunk to free up. So the command sent me to Philly for five weeks. Each day, I went into the office to check in, take out the trash, and go to my quarters for the rest of the day. It was pointless to me. The person I reported to was a friend, so I hatched a plan.

"Listen, I can call you to report instead of coming in. I'm going back south."

"Do what you want, but you're on your own if you get in any trouble, and your ass better call every morning too" he said.

I went back to North Carolina and chilled with my people, but I called my homie in Philly each day to ensure Navy life was secure. After two weeks, he alerted me that command was on the hunt for me that morning, so I hauled it back to Philly. Things weren't bad. The message was for me to join my ship in Charleston, South Carolina instead of Bahrain. Tasha and I purchased a single-wide trailer in Lumberton and pulled it to Charleston. I was married and nineteen, but I didn't know a damn thing about marriage. Tasha stayed home while I went to work on the base. We only had one vehicle, so it made sense for me to have it most days. My life didn't change too much. I was drinking with my friends at the white strip club, shooting pool, watching football at the sports bars, you know just being a dumb, immature husband.

My work hours on the Navy base were 11p.m. to 7a.m. One night, I kissed my wife at the time, Tasha, goodbye, and I made the thirty-minute trip to base, only to find my tire was flat as soon as I arrived. One of my buddies (the one who received the fake digits from Tasha by the way) ran me back home to get a spare. When we pulled up, the light in the living room was on. That was strange, I thought to myself. As I walked in I found the mirror Tasha always used to do her hair on the floor in the living room, and my heart sank into my stomach. That meant nothing like a kidnapping happened. She took the time to do her hair so her disappearance was on purpose. But the drive to base and back was about an hour, so where the hell did she go in that short amount of time? I remembered my man Walt saying to me he bet Tasha was in there knocked out and me answering yes. I knew it was not true, but the lie wasn't as bad as the truth. Truth was I had no idea where she was and it was killing me on the inside.

We went back to the base, and the entire time, I wondered where Tasha was. She didn't have any friends, and we didn't have family in the area. It felt like the car was behind a funeral procession because I couldn't get to that base fast enough. I changed that tire faster than a Nascar pit crew could do it, and I left without stepping foot on the ship. Finding out what my wife was doing became my number one priority. I got back somewhere around 1 am hoping that the situation had changed and this was going to be just some misunderstanding, but when I got back the circumstances had not changed. There was nowhere to go and check. Did I need to call the hospital? The police? What should I do? I settled on parking my Dodge in the empty lot across the street somewhat, hidden by the bushes, and just waited for her to get home.

That was a painful night, an unforgettable night. I can remember each painstaking minute that went by that night. From how quiet the beautiful, dark sky was to every song that played on the radio. Hour after hour after hour passed by. There went 2, 3, 4 and 5 a.m. Somewhere around 6 a.m. as the dawn began to bring light, a rust-colored Jetta with dark tinted windows and five-star rims pulled around the corner. As it inched closer my gut sank to an unbelievable low, I knew she was in that car. Then it stopped abruptly, they must've spotted me because the car suddenly went in reverse to make an escape.

The chase was on. We went through the city and hit the highway over 100 mph with my spare tire squealing and holding on for dear life. I snatched my gun from my glove box and started shooting at the Jetta. Three cop cars joined the fun, and a high-speed chase ensued. I was seeing red, so the cops didn't phase me, but the homeboy in the Jetta must've figured the police was his best option of getting away from me, so he pulled over. The next thing I knew, guns were pointed at me.

"Don't you fucking move! What the fuck is your problem?!" the older white Officer yelled while looking like his adrenaline was through the roof and he was ready to relieve that pressure.

I'm breathing heavily while tears flow down my cheeks, feeling schizophrenic and out of control. "I think my wife is in that car! I'll kill her and whoever is in the car with her!"

"You need to calm down! CALM THE FUCK DOWN!" he yelled. Officer two secured my weapon. "I will check that car, but you don't move from here."

A conversation started with the driver of the Jetta, but I couldn't see inside. Finally, the officer has the man step out. I can see him plainly today as I could that day. He was a dark-skinned brother with a low military cut with waves, and an Army sweatsuit. The dude exchanges words with the cop, and then they speak with someone in the car. The officer returns to my vehicle.

"Sir, you need to stay calm."

At this point I'm close to hyperventilating again as the blood rushes to my head because I feel like I know he's about to verify my thoughts. "She's in there, isn't she?! Aargh!"

Thoughts of running them down with my Dodge flood my mind.

"Sir, she's in there, but she's scared."

All I heard was confirmation, and rage mode was activated. My strength was so incredible that I could've killed the Hulk. The police had no choice but to handcuff me.

"You're not under arrest. We need to take you back to your ship," the officer said.

I returned to the ship in handcuffs, and the police had to explain the situation to my commanding officer. This meant the entire ship would now know my wife was with another man. I thought about my actions while being confined to my rack. I knew things could've been worse. The next day, my executive officer (XO) allowed me to go home to handle my business the right way.

"Do what's necessary to fix your home Taylor, but if I hear you did one thing, I'm gonna put your ass in the brig," XO said.

What seemed like anger to everyone was actually hurt feelings. Tasha was my wife, and I never expected her to do anything like this. She was an angel, my angel. Never in a million years would have I even suspected she was the type who would ever cheat. In my mind she was not even capable of following through with something so heinous. Marriage wouldn't have been considered if I thought Tasha was just another girl.

As a man most of us say, as did I, that I would kill somebody if I caught my wife cheating. But the truth is, you don't know what you will do when it happens to you. In fact, many of us say that with the thought in the back of our heads that we don't have to worry about it anyway because it will never happen to us. I think that day forever changed my view of marriage and the possibility of who will and who will not cheat. I went home with a broken heart but enough love to want to know why and how we could make this right. We hashed things out, and our emotions were all over the place. My biggest mistake during the conversation was asking her for the details surrounding the affair. I'll never ask another woman about the details. The memories of those details never go away, they haunt you forever.

What Tasha did was wrong, but our conversation uncovered my role in leading her to step out. Leaving her home day after day while I hung out with my guys was messed up. I left a lonely girl alone, and it turned against me. While I was out drinking and shooting pool, she was home bored and lonely, needing affection. I didn't take care of home, so somebody else did. Something I vowed to never let happen again. I always tell my younger guys to always take care of home first and listen to your woman and the clues she may give that she's vulnerable.

That same day my parents, who got word of the fiasco, drove all the way down from Lumberton to check on Tasha. They understood I had a temper and knew that Tasha's safety was the most important thing. As Tasha lay across the bed my mother peeped in and asked if she was ok. Once Tasha said yes they went back home knowing she was alive.

Infidelity didn't destroy us. We stayed together for eleven more years. Things weren't always great in our relationship, and both of us were to blame. Fights happened over stupid arguments, but we never pushed too much. The jealousy came close to taking me over the edge, but I was young and immature, and of course after the cheating I was very insecure. There was an incident where Tasha finally got a job that would take her out of the house and introduce her to people. Her new gig was at Taco Bell and I drove her on her first day. Everything was going great until this punk in the car next to us at a red light blew a kiss at Tasha. He really gonna do that shit in front of me like I won't handle that? I lost my damn mind and started another car chase with my gun in hand. She yelled no and told me to stop but her words fell on deaf ears. We made it to Tasha's job's parking lot with the police behind us with their weapons pulled out on me. Damn man, not again.

The police locked me up, but they let me go. I guess my jealousy and insecurity was a problem.

It came out once again at the Food Lion grocery store when a guy looked at my wife incorrectly and said something to her. I don't remember exactly what it was but I do know it was the wrong thing for him to say. We threw hands in the middle of the store. At that point and time I was about that life and didn't care about anything when I lost my temper. Gave him a two piece, and the dude surrendered in retreat. If Worldstar was a thing back then, I'm sure I would've gone viral a few times.

Death circled around once again while I was in the Navy. My grandfather, who everyone seemed to know, was the type of person to help those in need, or he would trust that borrowed money would have a return. He once let an Indian guy he knew hold some money while hosting a card game or something. Enough time had passed, but my grandfather didn't receive what was owed. The Indian guy came over knowing he owed, but he didn't offer a repayment plan or anything. My grandfather mentioned the money, and the Indian guy showed his anger by beating my grandfather to death by striking him in the head repeatedly. This happened in 1993, around the same time James Jordan, Michael Jordan's father, was murdered, which was only a couple of miles from my parent's house.

Tasha had to learn to deal with my bullshit, and I shamefully fell back into my bachelor ways when duty took me on deployment. I had the unbelievable experience of going through the Panama Canal, the very behemoth I read about in my Social Studies class. Wow what a thrill! I appreciate it even more now that I know exactly what was going on as we passed through.

USS Mahan passing through the Panama Canal

My shipmates and I were afforded liberty to see Panama City. Who knew I liked Spanish women? I didn't until

I got to Panama. I was all up in a spot called the Yacht Club, an on- the-water dance spot, eating fantastic food and consuming the best drinks. Let's just say the Spanish women love American sailors, and just like Michael Jackson said, "It doesn't matter if you're black or white! Hee hee!"

That wasn't the only fun spot we stopped at. The U.S.S. Halyburton had us docked in Ft. Lauderdale to lead the ceremony for the infamous around the world, Whitbread Race. Five of us rented a car, packed the trunk full of beer, and rolled around drinking until later that night when we headed over to Razor Ruddock's club, the boxer who got destroyed by Mike Tyson, called the Razor's Palace I think.

As we arrived at the club we were ecstatic and over-whelmed with how many women were in line to go in. We didn't even pay attention to the stares. We just figured they were looking because we were new faces and proba-bly looked like military guys. It wasn't long after we got inside that we noticed that strangely we were the only men in the building. That was strange, but we felt it was just our lucky night and that we hit the jackpot. But eventually we found the real reason we were so 'lucky'. It turned out it was a male revue night and the male strippers were on deck. As the music and show were about to begin and we were about to leave, the bouncer said, "Y'all not staying for the club part?" He continued to tell us after the male revue it turned back into a club as the men started to arrive. Now we started to think, "hmmm . . . if we stay the women will get all hot bothered by the show and look at us as their only choice to get lucky too." So we stayed.

The lights dimmed and the announcer said, "it's show-time," so we just hung at the bar and had some drinks. But the way the women were hooting and hollering I couldn't help but be intrigued by what the hell was going on. Now our plan worked to perfection, after the show was over, you could smell the aroma in the air. But let me tell you why.

First up, the announcer called out the Haitian Sensation. I chuckled, and it sounded more like a wrestler's name than a stripper's name. The guy was around 5'3 with a jheri curl, funny right? However he had something that intimidated men and women alike. He had a kickstand so long it was banging against his knee as he walked out. All I could think was, "What the hell is that?" and I'm so glad he's in Florida ruining marriages and not in that rust-colored Jetta I chased down.

Next there was Rico Suave, or something like that. Now this brother was smooth. He came out, took a young lady out of the audience, laid her down on the floor on a towel and then the song 12 Play by R. Kelly began to play.

By the time the lyrics got to 12, as you can imagine, the ladies were all hysterical and overheating. After the club part started we were able to get some numbers until it was over.

The next day we rolled down to Miami and somehow ran upon some "working" latinas. One of the dudes in our crew was notorious for saying, "white man this and white man that." He was cool, but a pain in the ass with all his preaching, so we nicknamed him Preacher Man. He never drank with us, but he was always buzzing around like a gnat telling us how unclean our bodies were with that poison we put in it. We wanted him to shut the hell up. All of us had a turn with a hooker, most of us for the first time, even Preacher Man. Apparently, the white man had nothing to do with hooker services. Preacher Man was last, and my man told him whatever he did, do not kiss the chick he was about to go in there with because her mouth had explored him south of the border. But poor ol 'Preacher Man came out of the room with lipstick smeared all over his mouth and face. We laughed until we cried.

Another deployment took me to GTMO in Cuba while on the U.S.S. Halyburton toward the end of my Navy career. Lord, it was hot as hell, but oddly enough it rained every day at two o'clock. I spent much of my time wearing a hand brace out to sea. The XO somehow thought (because I told him) I had injured my hand while loading missiles on board the ship. However, there is a good chance I hurt my hand while beating those two asses in Chicago. Either way, the XO said it had been too long, and that damn brace had to go when we returned stateside because we had to all be ready for this 6 month ship deployment, which is the ultimate sucks if you're in the Navy. We got back and the doctor checked me out. He started updating my medical record and said he needed to do one final X-ray.

The doctor walked in with a disappointed look on his face. "Taylor, I'm sorry because I should have run the x-rays sooner. You have arthritis in your hand. You have two choices. We can let it go and you can tolerate the pain and keep your Navy career. Or I have to do a carpal-meta-carpal fusion, which will force you out of the Navy."

"Doc, you're telling me I cannot go on this six-month deployment, gain disability, and have to get the hell out of the Navy?" I asked.

The facts were there, and I did my best to look sad, but my internal organs were doing the happy dance.

"Doc, I can't live with this pain anymore, uggggh where do I sign?"

I had the surgery, but my Naval career continued for another two years on light duty. I'm hard-headed sometimes, so I continued to play basketball after the surgery with the cast on my hand. My hand got infected, and half of my skin came off when the medical team removed the cast. The bone they fused broke off, so another surgery took place using a bone from my hip. Finally, I received my walking papers on November 15th, 1995.

Hitting The Weight Room Everyday

Back To Civilian Life

I got out of the Navy just in time to celebrate Thanksgiving. Tasha and I had thought about where we would live once I joined the civilian world but still had not settled on anywhere. All we knew is we wanted to leave Charleston.

We decided on Thanksgiving day that we would head to Chicago to visit her family, and lo and behold our Ford Escort broke down in a little sleepy country town called Camden, South Carolina, just two hours into our trip. There we were, stuck at a gas station parking lot, and it dawned on us that Camden seemed like a great place for a fresh start. The rest is history, and that's where we went after the Navy.

Before I left Charleston I was hired as a Summerville police officer but after taking my fingerprints they notified me my identity had been stolen in New York and until that was sorted out I couldn't be brought on. That was the hassle that prevented that career from happening. By the time we moved to Camden I was getting a monthly disability check from the Navy, but that wouldn't cut it, so I started working, trying to figure it out. At one point I was on my grind as a Kirby vacuum salesman. Blessed with the gift of gab, I went door to door and showcased the miracles of having a Kirby in your life. That was interesting and sounded good, but it's hard trying to convince folks to spend a thousand dollars on a damn vacuum, even if it does do everything like wash your car and cut your grass (I'm only kidding).

Eventually, I moved on to a rent-to-own job as an account manager. You either paid your bill, we worked out something, or I took back the property you thought was yours. My role in the company was high standing. I stayed at the top of the company's performance list, hitting bonus after bonus. I think that's where I first noticed how competitive I was.

In 1996, I met Hubert Pearson when he started doing rent- to-own together at First Choice Rentals, and we quickly became best friends. Hubert introduced me to his best high school friend Quincy Reddick, who became my other best friend, and that hasn't changed to this day. I'm a big guy, but these two brothers made me look like small potatoes. Hubert was around 380 pounds, and Quincy was 6'8 and 450.

"Lamont, you should do bouncing and bodyguarding with us," Hubert said. "We work for Tony's Bouncers and Bodyguards. It's a good hustle. You may have to bust some ass every now and then but it's not hard work."

I wasn't opposed to making extra coins on the side or frankly busting a few asses, so I went to a job with them one night. That first night was one hell of a job. We ended up running security for the No-Limit Records concert after party. You know Master P, Silkk the Shocker, Mia X, Mystical, and the whole damn crew were there. There were about twenty of us working security, and I felt like being the new guy I needed to show them I'm 'bout it, bout it.'

About six bouncers got into a verbal altercation with some dude. I knew this was my chance to do what I do. I didn't say a word, I just parted the crowd and walked up to the loudmouth and let my fist make an introduction. I hit him as hard as I could and watched him fall asleep before he hit the floor.

I remember Hubert yelling out, "Oh, shit, that's what I'm talking about!" All the bouncers were hyped! From that point I was trusted and treated like family. We were some natural bullies for these jobs, so we always anticipated a moment to mix it up. I was the smallest bouncer, but I was a quick-fuse time-bomb ready to beat the hell out of someone. Working as a bouncer and bodyguard made my nights exciting. What an adrenaline rush. The fights were epic, and the star connection created memories. I worked for K.P. & Envyi, Eric B. & Rakim, Jagged Edge, Gangsta Boo, and countless others. The most hectic night and fights probably happened when I worked for Goodie Mob. While working the Goodie Mob event, I beat this guy down, slapped the cuffs on and carried him out where I handcuffed him to the tour bus. Man that was a crazy night, fight after fight.

Some nights were really dangerous though, seriously. One night we were at a club and there was obvious tension between the bloods and crips. All I remember is when the fight broke out it became a melee. Quincy got hit with a flying champagne bottle and as the commotion spilled over into the parking lot were it sounded like we were in Vietnam. Assault rifles and pistols were being fired from all angles and all we could do was return fire and take cover.

Tony had us working all types of events and clubs, it wasn't long before we were doing security in strip clubs. Tasha knew my side job required me to frequent the clubs, but I purposely didn't mention what type of clubs. The Tony's Bouncers and Bodyguards staff were known for our skills and no nonsense approach, so we were in high demand at the most popular spot in Columbia, South Carolina at the time, Fantasy Island. Although it seemed as small as a large master bedroom, any and everybody that ran the streets frequented this joint. All the rappers came through Fantasy Island. I remember Atlanta rapper Drama showed up one night wearing a big-ass gold and diamond grenade around his neck. We knew when he came in with that shit on he wasn't safe. As expected, out of the blue a guy snatched the chain, and a few guys jumped Drama. My instinct was to help the rapper, not just because it was my job, but I also knew that they could very well kill him. You see during this time, Columbia was a killer's playground. Dangerous gives it no justice. So I jumped in and threw punches and covered Drama, who had been thrown into the small kitchen, to protect him.

"Lamont, are you alright?" Hubert asked.

"I will be once you get this nigga hands from around my neck!" I yelled.

Bottles and debris were thrown all around us. I could've lost my life that night over a chain that wasn't even mine. We worked those jobs for about $50, sometimes $40 a night. It wasn't worth the potential cost but hey, it gave me a legit reason to be in the streets making a few dollars. Gangs always showed up, knives and guns were always pulled out. I even saw someone catch five shots and lose his life at the door of Fantasy Island because the other guy didn't like what he said. It was too much. Damn.

Me And My Best Friend Quincy During Our Heaviest Days

These jobs weren't bringing in the necessary cash, and my marriage was in turmoil. Tasha's friends got on my damn nerves, and I knew it was a matter of time before they got into Tasha's ear and into some mess. Fantasy Island was an all- inclusive business, so there were nights when the ladies showed up for a good time. It was like a straight club inside the strip club. The straight ladies would come there to hang out too. If you think about it, it makes sense seeing as that's where all the dudes are. One night while working at Fantasy Island, a frantic Hubert walked over to me.

"Hey, J.D. said your wife just walked in," Hubert said.

I wasn't doing anything wrong, but Tasha would lose her mind if she knew I worked at Fantasy Island, but hold up, why the hell is she there? Anyway I hid all around the club and sometimes outside and just watched Tasha and her friends, being careful to make sure they didn't spot me. I went the entire night without Tasha finding out, but as they spilled into the parking lot to leave, this light-skinned brother named Carlos from Barnyard Entertainment crept up to Tasha's car. The calm brother I am, who can go from 0-100 real quick, grabbed my pistol and put one in the chamber. I was well aware of the Barnyard Entertainment crew and their reputation of getting it poppin' so I was ready for whatever.

I calmly walked over to the car and tucked my pistol in my pants, "Oh, this what the fuck we doing?" I asked.

"What are you doing here?" Tasha asked.

The dude, Carlos, looked surprised. "What's up, Big Man?" We knew each other from me working at the club.

"What's up? Fuck that. That's my wife. You tell me what's up," I said.

A pretty boy, light skinned dude tried to play it cool and brush everything off, but he didn't know me like that. I made sure the homie saw the gun.

"I'm gonna put two in yo ass and save seven for her trifling ass," I said.

Carlos told me to chill as he waved his hands in protest. The police were right across the street, but their presence didn't deter me from the madness. That's how it goes when I'm in a 'no fucks' mode.

"Tasha I'm saying this shit once, get your ass home," I said. She quickly tried to roll up her window, but with the barrel of my pistol peeping through and seeing my face filled with madness I guess she figured that wasn't a good idea. Instead of having her pull away, I jumped in her car and took her home.

That night didn't stop Tasha from messing with my emotions. On another night, just down the road from Fantasy Island, I was driving home with two other bouncers when I spot what looks like Tasha's car at another club. I was not going to let the disrespect fly, so we went in there so I could see if it's Tasha. Sure enough, I found her in the distance with one of her friends when she was supposed to be home. Oh yea she was trying me for real.

I rolled up, and before she noticed, I had Tasha suspended in the air by her neck. Now of course, I don't recommend or approve of violence against anyone, however there were some circumstances like this one where the ticking time bomb inside me caused me to lose all rationale and cross the line. So please don't make the mistakes I did many years ago.

Security rushed to the scene and said, "Lamont, yo let her go."

"Get your fucking hands off of me," I said. The local security teams knew my squad, and they didn't want those problems.

"We're only asking you to put her down. C'mon man you can't do this bruh."

I drove Tasha and her little friend home this time and cussed them out. Needless to say our relationship was growing very toxic and disrespectful. I just don't believe we were ever going to be back on track like we were before the infidelity. I no longer felt she was this flawless, perfect angel, in fact I think deep down inside I felt I was in love with a deceptive devil and I was still angry at myself for being that I. Adultery can ruin a marriage but do much more damage to an individual.

I was also working as a licensed security officer at different plants and warehouses. I was driving home one night in Camden, and my sleep apnea, which was getting worse and worse with the constant weight gain, stress, and lack of rest, had me drained for the night, so I pulled into a parking lot and fell asleep. An officer knocked on the window. My time as an officer afforded me the right to carry a gun, which I had in the car.

The officer said, "I see your gun's on the floor."

"Yeah, I'm so sleepy," I said. "I just finished my shift."

The officer wasn't hearing it, and he locked my ass up for not having the gun secured. I tried calling Tasha from jail, but she wasn't answering. The police released me the following day, but Tasha's location was mysterious. Finally, I got a call from one of her ratchet ass friends. The girl explained that Tasha was locked up in Columbia, and they tried reaching me all night. How the hell does a husband and wife go to jail on the same night in separate locations without knowing about the other? That gives you an idea of what the hell our lives looked like at that time. Tasha's reason for getting arrested was her fighting another girl at a club. I still don't feel like I know the entire truth of the story, but my hunch was there was a dude involved somewhere, at least that's what you think when you feel you're married to a lying, cheating devil. Then, she apparently talked some shit about being from Chicago to the police, and they gave her ass a Southern ass whooping. Never forget, it ain't where you from, it's where you at. Besides that's what she got for going out instead of staying at home.

We were no longer good together, and the bickering was pushing us toward separation. Not long after that, I became an assistant manager at Advanced Auto Parts while trying to move away from the rent-to-own business. I also went to Central Carolina to work on my associate's degree. Life was going well, but I couldn't keep my eyes off the beautiful women at my college. Hubert and I hatched an idea to start an adult production company using the college girls. Initially, we thought about having chicks doing pornos. I remember approaching one of the finer broads at the college with the jiggly booty and dropping some words on her that made her light up. I told her how she has the face and body of a goddess and how she was destined to be a well known superstar. Well one thing led to another and before you know it, she was buck ass naked on the bed putting on a show for our cameras.

But we eventually settled with Dark Man Productions, where we managed only exotic dancers. I mean it was easier because we already had a relationship with dancers from our work at Fantasy Island and we felt we understood their mindset.

Strip For Me

The start of my illustrious stripper management career began when I took ten dancers to a new club opening in

Greenwood, South Carolina. I remember looking back in my rear-view mirror and seeing like seven cars in a procession and thinking, "wow this is coming together." That night I told the gentleman acquiring my services that he had to give me $100 per dancer before I let the girls even get out of their cars. I had my assistant take the girls to the dressing room and when he told me they were dressed and ready, I entered and laid out the rules of Lamont to them. All eyes were focused on me. I was Big L, and I felt like the motherfuckin' man up in that piece. I sat down with a cigar and sipped on drinks while watching the girls I brought. I made the night happen, and the money was right. I thought to myself that a future in the stripper business was something I could get used to doing. Yeah I liked this lifestyle for real.

Pimpin Ain't Easy

My hustle came together, and before long, I provided dancers for lawyers, doctors, husbands, bachelors, even some Charlotte Hornets, and Green Bay Packers. The Hornets party took place somewhere around 1998-1999. I took two girls to the Sheraton, or maybe the Renaissance, I'm not quite sure, in Charlotte with me. Inside these ballers had food, a platter of weed, and a platter of cocaine. These parties were on a different level, and the girls had an opportunity to make some extra money with the "side deals." My concern wasn't with any deals they made while working as long as they consented, I received my negotiated amount, and they were safe.

I mentioned that my new jobs started before my separation from Tasha. Well one day, while I was working as the store manager at Advanced Auto, I had to open the store and count the register. It was about 8 a.m. when I received a call from my wife.

"Let me ask you a question," Tasha said. "Who is Strawberry, Luscious, Chocolate . . . "

How did Tasha know those names? Oh, shit, my phone! This conversation had to happen in person. I raced home so fast I think she was still reading names when I arrived. I had to have a fair shot at attempting to erase Tasha's doubt. "It's not what you think."

Tasha's face scrunched together. "Oh, hell no! You're fucking all them hoes!" she said with anger in her voice.

I eagerly shared the details of my business with Tasha and explained why she regularly received random $400 shopping sprees from me.

"Baby, we can do this together. I am not messing with these chicks. It's about the bread for me, not these broads. You can help me run this, manage the money, and be in charge," I said. Her eyes said two words, but Tasha's mouth spewed more.

"You either quit this bullshit, or we're done."

My ambition couldn't match my vows to Tasha. Ending my dealings in the stripper world became the second time I chose my wife over a lucrative career opportunity. One time as a bodyguard, I was approached to sign on as part of Patty Labelle's security team. The work would have lasted almost a year at $400 per day. I regret giving up that opportunity to work for my favorite female artist at the time, but I wanted to save my marriage. I became a consultant of sorts as I became a silent partner in the exotic dancer industry with my man Hubert on the side.

Timing is everything, and the rent-to-own business called for me to return with the promise of me running a store. I was training for the new position in Sumter, South Carolina. My reputation on the job, was as the guy who secured the hard to get accounts. Speaking is an asset, and I used the gift to get people to pay their bills. I was so good that sometimes people would even help me carry out their repossessed furniture. I did what was necessary to get my numbers noticed within the company, including waking kids up to snatch their bunk beds on a Saturday morning. It wasn't personal. It's never personal. To this day I tell my staff my work attitude is never personal. I don't like being an asshole to them, the same way I wouldn't want to take a kid's tv while he's watching Saturday morning cartoons. But that's business, not personal.

As good as I was at doing my job, there was one repossession that proved to be the biggest headache of them all. Barbara, the neighborhood crackhead, had a TV that she tried to keep without making even the first payment. Her ratchet ass made a down payment but then never made another payment again. Those accounts required the big dogs to take back the property. I told another guy to come with me, a jack-legged preacher who was holy as can be until he wasn't. "No one has ever caught up with Barbara. Today, it's going to get done," I said. I had no idea that day would impact the rest of my life.

I knocked on the door. "Barbara, listen I know you're not a bad person. Return the TV now, and you'll be able to rent from us again. We won't hold this against you."

Repo-Preacher man laughed at me, but Barbara soon opened the front door, leaving the screen between us.

"Well, can I come in?" I asked. I only needed to get inside because our chances of getting the tv increased tenfold. Barbara agreed to let me in so we could discuss the rental agreement. I heard her yell to her teenage son upstairs so I knew she wasn't alone. My way with words pulled Barbara in, and she understood the television couldn't stay in her possession. However, the weather didn't cooperate with the truck we chose to utilize that day. The television would've been ruined by the rain. Barbara was on our side, but she was a jittery crackhead, which made her unpredictable. I broke it down for Repo-Preacher. "Go back and bring the van before we lose this tv."

Barbara was a well-known crackhead in Sumter who hung around Noons Cafe, a local spot for drug dealing. Keeping her engaged in a long conversation while Repo-Preacher went to get the van was only achievable because of my charm. We finally got the tv, and we went back to the office. I finally did what no other employee could do before, close Barbara's account. A week later, I was running the Monday morning employee meeting when I notice two plain-clothes officers and two in uniform entering the store.

One of the officers asked if I was Lamont Taylor. "Yes, I'm

Lamont," I said.

"We need you to put your hands behind your back."

"Whoa Whoa Whoa . . . for what!" I said in disbelief at what was happening.

The police cuffed me in front of everyone and led me to their car.

"Can you tell me why you're arresting me?" I asked.

The female detective stared at me and sternly said, "Sir, you're being arrested for criminal sexual conduct in the first degree."

My ears didn't understand the language the detective spoke. Who the hell did I piss off for my name to be slandered in the worst way possible? "From who? What are you talking about?" This has to be a mistake.

"It will be explained to you later, Sir."

The officers took me to the station for booking. The arrest happened on a Friday, so I had to wait until Monday before anything could happen. The cell conditions were below the standards of a rat, and I had to sleep on the floor because the two beds were occupied. "I have to warn y'all, I snore."

One of my cellmates laughed and said, "Shit, I've been here nine muthafucking months. I've heard it all." The following day, the guy was singing a different tune. "Yo, CO, this nigga gotta go, bruh."

I finally got out, but life had drastically turned against me. My car was impounded, my job fired me, the house was in default, and the news was the straw that broke my marriage's back. I received the paperwork that detailed the charges against me, and to make matters worse. Barbara, the crackhead, had accused me of coercing her into performing oral sex on me. Listen, I'm no angel by any means but this shit just wasn't true and Barbara's actions were those of a crackhead. My anger and disbelief were that the police knew of Barbara's reputation and chose to pick her side instead of remaining impartial.

My job said they would look into the allegations and waited weeks before firing me. I was in the storm because I did a job that they wanted me to do, and I did it well. Then, those people dared to treat me like a criminal. I worked my ass off doing things the right way for a company that only saw me as a number. They tossed me out like I meant nothing to them the second I stopped producing.

I moved back to North Carolina, and I could only afford a public defender. The system was so backed up that I drove to South Carolina for court roll calls every two months to see if my name was on the day's docket. Understand, my freedom relied on the courts. I mean, I knew I was innocent but I had no faith the South Carolina judicial system would find a black man innocent of anything. So I knew if my name was called on the docket that day, there was a real chance I would never go home again.

A prestigious Camden lawyer told me those charges in South Carolina demanded a 35-year sentence with a possibility of parole after serving 32 years. My life was in turmoil for a year and a half. Thoughts of physical shackles followed any moments of laughter, but mental freedom had already been stripped from me because my life was on hold.

One day I tried to make the routine trip for a roll call, but I suffered a flat tire. My mother worked at our local courthouse, so I went there to seek guidance. She suggested we go to the judges' chambers to call the Sumter courts. I provided my credentials over the phone.

The clerk said, "Oh, your case has been dropped."

"Wait, please check that again. I don't want to have a warrant because I failed to show," I said.

"No, I'm looking at your file. Your case has been dropped for insufficient evidence." A note was attached to my file that stated Barbara made the story up.

Tears filled the room as the weight of the world was lifted from my shoulders. I hugged my mother, and I vowed to turn my life around. I called my public defender because the clerk of courts said my case was dismissed over a month before. This dude could barely remember my name all of the other times we met.

"Sir, the clerk said my case was dismissed a month ago," I said.

"Oh, congratulations!"

I wish I could've had the conversation in person because this guy was missing something. "Why didn't YOU tell me?"

"I didn't know! I have a caseload of fifty defendants. I don't look at a case until the day that client has court."

The injustice that happens to people in my predicament is a travesty. South Carolina will make an arrest, book you, and then investigate, whereas at least North Carolina investigates, builds evidence, and then arrests. At the time, I had lost everything because the system failed me.

Years later, I went to expunge my record. The black woman helping me out said she saw a marijuana charge listed on my record. I don't smoke. I didn't then, I don't now, and I never will. My taste for alcohol was always undeniable, but I was about the only person in my crew going back to high school who left drugs alone. The charge was egregious.

The clerk said, "Listen, I'm taking this charge off your record because I believe you, and you aren't the first person I've heard this about."

I never would've known about the drug charge if I hadn't fought to clear my record, and the fight came about because I wanted to be the business instead of being in business. I wondered how many individuals carried un-warranted charges through life.

Looking For Love In All The Wrong Places

Snatching my life back from the clutches of jail pushed me to change, but it also increased my appetite for the goodies I had been missing since losing everything. My reintroduction to the dating world wasn't as glorious as expected. Maybe the game had changed since my foray into marriage. Live Links, a hookup site over-the-phone type company, also fed into my addiction to playing the field. Those commercials had the lines, "They're out there. Singles who live where you do. Who thinks like you do and are ready to make a real connection. On Live Links, we give your voice more choice." I wanted all of the choices. These weren't sex lines. You spoke with real women in your area.

One night, I conversed with this sweet sexy voiced woman over the phone. She said, "I'm short, but my body is banging." Live Links already scored me the digits, so the next move was to get to the smashing. Shorty lived al-most three hours away in Augusta, Georgia. It was 11:30 p.m., but the girl said everything to let me know I had her if I wanted her. This was too easy. My cousin stayed with me at the time, so I made him roll with me for the drive. We hauled ass to Augusta. She and I were on the phone as

I got close to the house so she could guide me in. I drove into her yard, and the headlights shined on the chick. My cousin started laughing, and I could see why. The girl was a little person, a dwarf, a damn midget! It didn't seem real.

She was 3'10, at best, with a tiny burnt-up arm that flapped out of control. The situation was unlike anything I had ever witnessed. However, I drove a long-distance thinking about getting busy with her, and at this time, it is what it is. I mean, shit she was short but she was right, she did have a banging little phat booty though. I hit it all over that living room and left an hour later, and my cousin laughed all the way back to North Carolina.

That was a crazy phone link but it wasn't my last. I hit up Live Links again, connecting with a piece from Fayetteville, North Carolina. Her voice showed she was a little older than me, but I don't mind exploring the primed and ready ones, if you remember my teenage years. I suggested an evening of entertainment. She responded, "I can stay out up until eleven."

I didn't know what she meant, but I figured the old girl wanted to get back home at a decent time. I pulled up to the address she gave me, but the place was a facility instead of a house. The sign out front indicated it was a rehabilitation center, and I was thinking "what in the hell?" Maybe she was getting ready to get off work? But hey I showed up with a goal, so I wasn't turning around. I strolled up to the front desk and asked for Cecelia.

The nurses started hooting and hollering, "Ooh, Cecelia has a date!"

I should've known right then something was off. Cecelia walked around the corner holding a woman's arm. I saw Cecelia smiling, but her ass doesn't see me. She's blind. I'm talking Stevie Wonder blind. I could leave, but I'm here now, besides I didn't want to hurt the old gal's feelings. The nurse hands Cecelia off to me, and I guide her to my truck. We go back to my place, sip on some wine, and have a few laughs. She's not that attractive, but hey at this point who cares. My hand reaches to turn the lights down low, but then I'm like for what? Cecelia can't see shit, no way. I decided to be butt-ass naked and be myself. Cecelia was old school, and she wanted to be wined and dined, but I was like, take your panties off granny. She was like 48, and I was in my late 20s. I smashed it and couldn't wait for the sun to rise so I could take her ass home.

Chapter Five

THE ROLLERCOASTER OF LIFE IS A BIT OVERWHELMING

THE COST OF CHANGE

I always felt like I was different and elite. Whether I was in the Navy, doing rent-to-own, bouncing, or in the stripper business, I always felt like I was the man, should be the man, or could be the man. I don't know if it was because my mother instilled in me at an early age that I can be great at anything I wanted to, or if it was all those Saturday mornings of watching Ric Flair proclaim, "In order to be the man, you have to beat the man, and I am the man! Wooo!"

Getting back focused was a little difficult once my marriage to Tasha ended and everything was taken from me. Looking back, I think I was depressed. But back in those days, depression wasn't discussed, especially in the African- American community. That's when the real weight gain started. I was finding comfort in food to take my mind off being sad or lonely. Along with that "comfort" came the insecurity that soon followed. As the weight piled on, the feelings and insecurities would take me back to my childhood when the teasing from kids and adults alike about my weight would bring me down. Whether I was called fat, chubby, heavyset, or my personal favorite, husky. Hell I'd rather be called fat than husky. I mean what the hell is a husky anyway? And the fact at that time they had a section in the department stores that said husky, are you kidding me?

My Heaviest Weight In The Early 2000's

Somewhere along the way, I developed sleep apnea and the weight gain probably worsened the effects ten times. The inability to rest at night because of the restricted breathing caused a different type of snoring. I mean the type of snoring that sounded like a freight train. Of course, this kept me from enjoying the small things in life. I didn't go out to the movies for over a decade because I couldn't keep my eyes open much past the opening credits. Once the popcorn was gone it was a wrap. It was embarrassing having my date wake me up once the movie had finished. This is after jabbing me 25 times before giving up and letting me sleep.

My condition was also dangerous. I wrecked four cars because I fell asleep while driving. I can't tell you how many times I would get the horn blown at me at a red light because I had dozed off. I once got a job to watch after a troubled teen at his middle school but that didn't last long. In fact, I was fired the first week. Everything was all good at first. I just sat in the back of the class and played on my phone or whatever. No biggie. Well, panic struck me when on my second day at work, a substitute was there for the day and she said the class was going to watch a movie. Ugh oh, you mean the lights are going to be turned off and we're about to watch *Matilda*? I already knew what it was, lights out for me for real. Needless to say they fired me that day for being a distraction. Evidently it was hard for them to hear the tv in the front of the class when I was in the back cutting down trees.

My gift of gab pushed me to become one of the top car salesmen at two dealerships, Honda and Toyota. But each position was lost because I couldn't be trusted to do test drives or stay awake during downtime. Can you imagine walking in a car dealership and one of the car salesmen is stretched out snoring and then asks you to go hop in for a ride?

At this time I had been found eligible for disability from the military but only twenty percent. That was barely enough to keep rent paid anywhere or gas in my hooptie ride. I was broke. I was embarrassed to be broke. I felt like a failure. I was in the military and got out only to land on my feet. Sure I could have gone back to my parents, who would've gladly taken their only son in and helped him get on his feet. But that would've come with a price. No matter how old you are when you live under someone else's roof or they're providing you with meals, you have to live by their rules and listen to the advice they will give you daily. That wasn't going to happen. I had been on my own since I raised my hand to go into the Navy at the age of seventeen. I was just going to have to figure it out.

It was when, one night, I only had a can of green beans in the cabinet to eat that I realized I had hit rock bottom. My last resort was to sign up for food stamps at 28 years old. Just being in that office providing them with every little detail of my life just so I could get food was disgraceful and humiliating. I told myself I never want to go through this again. It took something from me. I never forgot that feeling and it keeps me motivated every single day.

Soon after I met my cousin Tonia's neighbor, Linda, who had just moved down south from Newark, NJ. She was a half Puerto Rican and Dominican woman who was mad cool. She was smart, funny, pretty, and we vibed really well together. Linda suffered from Multiple Sclerosis, making it difficult for her to walk on her own. Linda had five kids (Manny, Tiffany, Timothy, Linda, and Ynez), and hanging with her and the kids kept me going. I felt accepted, and Linda's bunch became my adoptive kids in a way. Doctor appointments, schooling, and activities kept me busy. My love for that family took me on trips to Newark whenever Linda needed to go home. For a couple of years Manny even moved in with me. He only needed some extra guidance and discipline like all teenagers do. He was my son then and to this day is like a son to me. The love I had for them and they had for me pulled me out of the darkness. It's good to see them all grown up on Facebook. All the kids now have their own kids and I get a kick out of watching them all. Although I haven't seen Linda in a while outside of social media, my love and appreciation for her will never waver. She helped me in ways that I needed and no one else could or tried to. I love her dearly and she will always remain one of my best friends.

SOUTH OF THE BORDER

Spending so much time with Linda's family pushed me to better my situation. Before long, I entered a familiar world when JD, a cat I worked with at the strip club, Fantasy Island in Columbia, said he was opening up a strip club called Reflexxions near my hometown. "Lamont, you know the girls, the game, and you were a bouncer. I need your help."

This was around November 2000, and the location was in Dillon, South Carolina, close to a place everybody traveling I-

95 knows, where North and South Carolina meet, called South of the Border. Close to fifty girls entertained on opening night, and thirty of them came from me and my connections. The environment was wild for most, but only business for me. I spent so much time working in and around strippers that I could separate myself from the attraction. I tell people that I've seen so many booties and boobies in my life that it takes more than her appearance for her to be sexy to me. Anyway, the money started

rolling in, and I began dabbling a little into managing girls like before, but one incident halted all that.

A guy close to 50 Cent (Curtis Jackson) came in by himself one night, and we started conversing over several bottles of Cristal he purchased. He looked like he had bread. He was driving a Mercedes truck with the Gucci interior and had a toy poodle in the car with him that had on a Gucci sweater. The guy said, "Hey, send me one of your best girls down to Miami, and we'll work something out. The clubs in Miami are jumping and we both can make some money." I chose one of my most popular girls, Juicy, to take the trip and earn the extra money. Juicy was pretty, 2 Live Crew thick, and redboned, so she would excel in Miami. Almost a week passed by without me hearing any-thing, but then Juicy called and woke me up around 3 a.m., hysterical one night.

"Lamont, this is Juicy. You have to get me out of here."

"Where are you?"

"I'm still in Miami. Get me out of here. This dude's a pimp and he's crazy!"

My resources brought Juicy back home, and she was relieved. Juicy said as soon as she met the guy in the airport parking lot he said, "break yourself." In the hood that means give me everything you got. He snatched her phone and money, placed Juicy in a house with seven other girls, and started grooming her for the pimped out lifestyle. Nowadays it's known as human trafficking. One of the girls at the club felt sorry for Juicy because she didn't fit the profile of a professional, so she slipped her a phone. I put Juicy in a situation that could've cost her life. My role in dancer management before never entered the realm of pimpin', and I wasn't about to start either. The decision to leave that world was final. The universe tried to tell me to go before the Juicy chaos, but I didn't listen. Now Juicy's kids could have lost their mom for the love of money and greed. I was a badass but I have also always had a conscience for doing the right thing.

One evening, while I was working security at the front area of the club, a big-time local drug dealer showed up. They called him " No.1 Stunna." He was an Indian guy who was used to getting what he wanted. We all knew him because he would come in sometimes, and for the most part he knew all of us. On this particular night he showed up with a lady, and she didn't have identification. I had been given strict orders to tighten up entry and ID everybody I didn't know personally or hadn't been there before.

"She needs ID," I said.

No.1 Stunna looked at me and snarled, "It's in the truck, man. You know me. You're gonna make me go back to the truck?"

"You're right, I know you but I don't know her. She's going to have to show me some ID. Not my rules my man I'm just doing what I was told."

He thought his pampered ass would receive star treatment, but I'm not everyone else. I followed the rules, and No.1 Stunna went and grabbed the girl's ID. He looked at me sideways when he reentered, but that comes with the territory. He rocked with his crew all night, but he stared me down as they left.

"That's fucked up, man," No.1 Stunna said.

"What are you still mad about, bruh? You went in, and y'all had a good time," I said.

"That's fucked up."

He drove off in his truck and I thought that was the end of it. But near closing time, as I was wiping down the mirrors by the register. I noticed a white guy enter. "Hey, we're closed."

"You're closed?"

"Yeah, we close at 4," I said. My movements returned to my task, but my eyes never left the mirror. Ever since my days of working my first bouncer job, I learned to always watch my surroundings. This guy pulled out a hawkbill knife, a long switchblade with a hook at the end. I turned and dipped back as the blade came narrowly close to my throat. He made an incision from the top of my chest to my navel. The heat from the knife released the old me, and I was instantly on top of him beating the shit out of him. The owner and other security rushed out and pulled me off the guy, letting him run out the door and not realizing what had happened. I remember hearing one of them yell that I was sliced open. It was then I noticed the blood flowing everywhere. They wanted to take me to the hospital, but hey, as I told you I was a badass so I ignored their advice and drove myself to the hospital. I remember it took 101 staples to close me up.

We saw the guy run up the road to the No.1 Stunna's truck. That's how we knew this attempt to end my life was a hit job. I grew up fighting, but I never expected to take things too far. For the first time in my life, I contemplated killing another person. A call was made to a cousin in Charlotte to put things in motion. We knew where No.1 Stunna lived, so we staked- out a plan. My cousin was down, and never been afraid to let off that heat. I don't go past one-on-one at my core, so I pulled the call. I had to believe that karma would do justice although I must say I always wanted payback.

Well, eventually, like most all drug dealers, No.1 Stunna went to jail, and someone snatched his life. It was a cut job from his neck to his navel, and rumor has it, his guts were on display. Rumors also spread that I made payback arrangements because of the similar ways he and I were cut when he was killed . . .

At that juncture in my life I was at the point where being better is a priority, but situations continued to test me and worked my last nerve. I was driving in a small town, and a white officer pulled me over and offered zero reasons for why. Everyone knows that the law says we have rights, but not everyone realizes that color factors into who actually has rights, especially in the south. The police searched my Oldsmobile and tore it apart, literally. They pulled everything out of the trunk and the glove compartment, looked under the hood, and even took my seats out of the car. There wasn't anything to find, but they tossed everything onto the side of the road and left it there for me to clean up. No explanation whatsoever, no apology, no nothing. You could look in their faces and see the disdain for me. They wanted me to feel like I was still a nigger to many, and it wouldn't change no matter what status you have, education you obtained, or money you made. Nope, you were still a nigger. Unfortunately, I've had my car searched probably six or seven times in my life. Never found anything, but for some reason I looked like I probably had something. Wonder what that look is?

Even though money still has to be made, I no longer wanted to be in dangerous situations. Somewhere around 2002, I started going to New York City about every two weeks to secure more items for my street hustle. I would sell my product at clubs and industrial plants, but my biggest profits came from the flea market where I paid my cousin Bobby to make the sale. My merchandise consisted of bootleg CDs & DVD's, knock off purses, copyright infringed clothing like ENYCE, Baby Phat, and Phat Farm, and anything else that could be flipped for a quick turnaround profit. I was your modern day hustle man.

My boy, Score, was my protégé, and was always with me for the ride. All the movies on DVD would only cost me a dollar, and I would sell them for $10, so I was killing the game. I mean don't let a Tyler Perry movie come out or something else in high demand, like The Passion For The Christ or The Lion King; money, money, money! This was better than being a drug dealer. We would go to the garment district on 34th and Broadway and link up with the Africans who ruled the street bootlegging game. I swear every one of those dudes was named Jallo.

One time Score and I were directed to a giant storage warehouse in Harlem, filled with porn. Out of all of the items I sold, porn was by far the most lucrative, to the point that customers called me the 'Porno King.' We made the journey from North Carolina to New York City non-stop. There were times I would leave home around midnight and be at the spot by nine, finished and back on the road by ten, bumping Teddy Pendergrass and R. Kelly all the way. Bootlegging is illegal, but it's as normal as waking up.

Our problems with the police stemmed from the constant stops to perform drug and gun searches. We were stopped on more than one occasion by the cops who would toss our bootleg items on the side of the road, but strangely enough they never confiscated them. I guess that's small potatoes and they wanted the big fish.

It wasn't all work and no play though. We made sure to stop and check out the different strip clubs and nightclubs to see what other states had to offer. Score would always say I love getting into some shit, so there's no surprise that one night when we stopped at Club Baltimore I was supplied with some classic shit-stirring. My time as a bouncer kept me on my toes and my mind focused whenever I stepped foot inside a club. Never have my back to the door, pay attention to the tone of the club, know where the exits are, you know things like that.

"Score, I think these guys are about to get into it."

"So, it doesn't got shit to do with us," Score said. "Stay out of it, Superhero!"

Just as my Spidey sense predicted, a fight broke out, and I got involved. Bodies flew around, punches were getting thrown, and the mayhem was out of control. The cops started breaking it up, but those of us in the thick of it continued brawling outside. My eyes connected with Score through a window because he's still inside, and his shrug and perplexed stare at me said it all. Why the hell was I fighting with people I didn't even know? True to how Score viewed me, I put on my cape and tackled a guy running full-speed toward a female cop. Some of the police thanked me for getting involved. Stopping shit from escalating was always in me. Maybe it was the thrill of watching a guy get his karma by getting his jaw rocked. Not sure, but oddly enough I enjoyed it.

After a night of security at Reflexxions, I would usually go to

Waffle House with Score, to talk to my friend Jo, one of my favorite waitresses. One night a New York City pimp named Half left the club and was at Waffle House with three of his girls. Now Half was about 5'0, so I'm assuming that's where he got his nickname from. You know, like half a man. Anyway he knew me and I knew him. No animosity or friendship, we just would see each other at the club but never really had a conversation before. One of the girls asked Half if she could eat some cake. In the traditional pimp world, the girls needed permission for everything. I was tired, and was in jerk mode.

"Yo, Score. This bitch has to ask him if she can eat some cake! That's some stupid shit," I said. What I heard come out of my mouth sounded funny, but I was serious.

"Yo, Lamont, chill on that," Half said.

"Fuck what you talking about, and fuck that big-headed stripper bitch," I said.

Half tried to play it cool, but I was messing with the man's reputation in the streets, so he had to press me, especially in front of his girls.

"Lamont, what's up with that, man?" Half asked.

I stood up and pointed at the group. "Fuck you and them bitches! I'll fuck all of yo asses up!" I said. Every person in my area was in trouble when my temper became active. Score knew not to intervene when my mood didn't agree with the environment.

"Yo Score, get your man!" Half said.

Score shrugged and tried to ignore the stress I had created. I towered over Half in bully mode, and every word that rolled off of my tongue disrespected his lifestyle. The details from that night are shareable, thanks to Score. I didn't remember too much of anything from that night until Score later reminded me.

Six months later, I went to New York City by myself. I got the bootleg goods and did a little shopping for my-self. As I was walking up the street to my car by Madison Square Garden a white Lexus truck pulled up on me.

"Yoooooooo!"

My attention turned to the man shouting from the Lexus. It's Half. The events from when we last interacted didn't register, so I strolled over full of excitement to see a familiar face in the big city. "Yo, what's up, Half." My fist stretched out to exchange pounds. Half obliged, but confusion joined his awkward display. We talked for a bit, but Half never addressed the argument at Waffle House and hell I didn't remember it so it was the unbeknownst to me, elephant in the room. I called Score during the drive back down south.

"Yo you'll never guess who I ran into in New York," I said. "Who?" Score asked.

"Half !"

"Oh, shit. What happened?! Everything cool?! You alright?!" "We chopped it up for a few, that's about it."

"Nigga, last time we saw Half you cussed his little ass out," Score said. "You're lucky that nigga didn't pop you."

Sleep apnea affects memory in extreme cases. I had no recollection of my beef with Half until Score made me aware. My excitement to see a familiar face probably saved me that day.

(R.I.P. Jo)

The bootlegging business was booming, so I focused on selling my merchandise outside the clubs. I stepped away from bouncing, which paid peanuts compared to what I was making on the streets. I met this dancer at Reflexxions who was a newbie in the strip clubs. Her name was Sherlene and she enticed me into breaking the stripper code. My number one rule was never, and I mean never date the dancers. At first, her deep story made me want to help her break free of the mental jail her past put her in. Sherlene's father used to sell her off to his friends when she was younger. Tell me that shit wouldn't mess with the mind of any young girl who looked up to her father. Oddly enough, she still yearned for the love of her father. Unfortunately, this horror led her to alcohol and drug abuse.

I did my best to support Sherlene and her daughter. They even moved in with me as we started a relationship. And for the most part we had fun, of course whenever the depression and addiction didn't intervene. It was a cycle of highs and lows. She would fall into a state of depression that was accompanied by late night screams out of her sleep, and days of disappearing to get high. I tried to be there but she was all over the place and it just wasn't working. We broke up, and she passed away in her sleep three years later. With the unhealthy relationship I have with death, you have no idea the thoughts I have about Sherlene and if I could have done something more to help her. She might still be alive. I think about her often. Not in the traditional way of missing a girlfriend, but more so my memory of her love for her daughter and how she wanted to protect her from the things she went through. She would cry and say she didn't want to die young, but she did.

Not too long after Sherlene and I broke up I went with

Quincy to a bar in Lumberton and ran into my childhood neighbor. As we were talking and catching up, a young, slim, dark-skinned girl caught my attention.

"Yo, who is that?" I asked.

My neighbor rolled his eyes. "That's my stupid ass baby mama," he said.

"Oh, damn my bad dawg," I said.

My neighbor waved off my words. "Naw, fuck that bitch. You can have her. That's just my baby mama. I can't stand her ass!"

Giving me the green light to holla at your baby moms is a mistake. I gave shorty the eye, she gave the I'm wit' it look and we exchanged digits. My night was over as far as I was concerned. I was drunk and tired so I went home while Big Q went to an afterparty. He called me and said he saw the new chick at the party and she was talking his ear off asking about me. After a quick conversation, the girl was at my spot. I don't remember much outside of me being extremely drunk and what attracted me to her at the club, that slim, thick lil booty. I do remember us being in my bedroom with the lights down low and she slowly got undressed. When she pulled down the jeans the girl's body revealed she had a damn butt pad on. Wait, what the hell! My mind went blank after seeing the chick's body wasn't hers, I think I just passed out.

I woke up the next morning believing we didn't get down and I missed my opportunity. I didn't even remember her leaving. Fast forward six months later, I was feeling good and social. I convinced Quincy and my cousin Bob to get together and have a small cookout. Nothing too special. We could fire up the grill, get some drinks, and invite a small crowd and play some cards. Shorty from the club came to mind.

"It's Lamont. We're having a get together at my place. You should bring a friend or two and swing by," I said.

"That sounds nice. I've been meaning to call you anyway. I need to tell you something," Shorty said.

I thought nothing of it. A couple of hours later there was a knock and the door opened, and in walked Shorty from the club. I looked at my boys, and their eyes grew large as they looked back at me. Shorty walked toward us with an obvious baby bump. She grabbed my hand and led me toward my bedroom.

Shorty couldn't stop grinning. "I just want to tell you we're having a baby!"

I shrugged. "That's awesome. You and who?"

Her laugh was disturbing, almost Dr. Evilish. "Me and you, silly!"

Hold up. I pressed pause on the panic button because I knew we had never had sex. I'm the guy who sexes up little people and serves the blind, so it wasn't me trying to deny the truth at all. "Are you sure? Cuz we never . . . "

"Yes we did, don't you remember?" she interrupted.

I didn't remember shit, so I couldn't really dispute her claims. But never have I been so drunk I couldn't remember knocking the boots. A baby was coming, and I had to step up. There's not an option not to. My first call was to my mother to break the news. Irene's only child was turning her into a grandparent, but the excitement never entered her voice. It didn't matter because there were only three months before my child would arrive, so I worked and saved and gave the baby mama money. Whatever shorty asked for, she received. Late night runs to the convenience store, she got it. She had enough pickles and peanut butter to last a lifetime.

My phone rings one day, and it's shorty telling me my baby is at the hospital. That's weird. She never even let me know she was in labor or anything. Thoughts of being a father pushed away any confusion. I was excited. Big L was about to be a dad, but it would be some time before the kid could go home because he was sick.

"Quincy, let's roll to the hospital. I want to see my baby," I said. We made the 45 minute drive to Fayetteville, and I found the Neonatal Intensive Care Unit area (NICU). Nervousness took over from the anticipation of laying eyes on my baby boy for the first time. As I prepared to check into the NICU, the nurse in the area had zero smiles.

The nurse stared at me up and down. "How may I help you?"

"I'm here to see my baby!" as I told her the name to look for.

"I'm sorry, but only the parents are allowed to go in."

My smile widened at the thought of being a parent. "I know.

I'm the dad of Shaquille."

The nurse didn't know what to think, but she could tell I believed what I had said. She informed me that Shaquille's parents literally just left and pointed to their names in the sign-in book. Wait so you mean to tell me the last few months were dedicated to providing for a child that wasn't mine? Naw, there had to be a mistake. I called the baby's mother and you could tell in her voice she didn't care, so I eventually told her I hope she rots in hell.

But wait, this story isn't over . . .

Fast forward seven months later, my cousin knocked on my bedroom door and woke me up while I was in bed napping with Sherlene, who had returned with the promises of getting clean and doing right. (I even attended AA meetings with her so I believed at that time she really wanted a change.) Anyway my cousin handed me a note that was placed on my windshield. The message was from Shaquille's mom, apologizing and explaining that she messed up bringing the other guy to the hospital and that I was Shaquille's real father. She said the baby resembled me, acted like me, and even inherited my asthma. And as much hurt and disappointment that situation had originally brought to me, deep inside there was still this want for me to be in the boy's life.

Not too long before all this drama, Sherlene and I had just got back together. She was absolutely devastated by the news because we had danced around the idea of having kids, and she wanted to be the person who gifted me my first child. She cried and she cried and she cried. There wasn't much I could do at the moment other than take care of my responsibilities. Too many games had been played for me to just accept Shaquille without taking measures to make sure he was mine so I ordered an online DNA test. I was able to convince the boy's mom I wanted to spend quality time with the little fella when really I wanted to get in that mouth. I swabbed the hell out of his mouth like I was checking for gingivitis. The results came in, and just as my mother suspected, the boy really wasn't mine and this was final. Yes it hurt to know I had been played yet again, but at least I found out before 18 years of child support. This time I called the child's mother with no pity.

"This is to be our last convo. I have proof if you want to see it. He's not mine. Don't call me any fucking more." She got the hint, and I never heard anything about her or Shaquille ever again.

My focus turned back to pushing my merchandise. One night, like I did every Saturday night, I had four tables set up at The Cage, a popular nightclub up the street from Reflexxions. Everyone knew who I was, and I always kept a few of my girl friends with me to keep me company and help guide the customers to my tables. One night, this guy left a drink on my table, violating one of my rules. A spilled drink doesn't pair well with CDs and DVDs, the plastic covering gets all sticky and everything. So while talking to a friend, I noticed the cup on my table. I didn't see whose it was and didn't care honestly, so I tossed it.

This drunk guy came over. "Hey, have you seen my drink?"

"Oh, my bad my brother. I didn't know it was your drink. I saw it on my table so I threw it away." I was cordial as I always am, until pushed to a point.

Drunk Guy nodded his head. "Cool. No problem, I guess you're buying me another muthafucking drink."

My reason for being there was to conduct business, but this guy's mouth was starting to annoy me. "Look, champ,

I ain't buying you shit." Drunk Guy decided he was on one and proceeded to bump the hell out of my table, causing my movies and CDs to knock over. His boy watched everything go down and rushed over to smooth things out.

"My bad dawg, my man just drunk. Sorry about that."

Our exchange of words was respectful, and he removed his friend from my area. I walked around the table and straightened up the mess Drunk Guy had created. Then I heard his annoying little voice.

"Nah, FUCK this muthafucka. He's gonna buy me a drink because he threw it away."

It was too late. I switched from businessman to ass-whooping man and WHACKUP, before I knew it, I punched ol' boy in the face. I dropped his ass and proceeded to beat the shit out of him. Security didn't know I was handing out the punishment, so they started hitting me. A voice yelled out, "Stop. That's the DVD guy." Security stopped, let me go, and began whooping Drunk Guy ass before dragging him out. A little while later, the police came in and pulled me outside for a talk. My boy, Chal, a deputy, showed me the warrant for my arrest because Drunk Guy was pressing charges. I used my connections with JD, the strip club owner across the street, to settle matters. He made one call, and the police ripped up the warrant.

The clubs weren't the only scene for supplying my customers. I also had flea markets on lock. Outsiders would've banked on me being a drug dealer with how much money I moved around. I had an acre of land with a flossed-out double-wide home with a huge living room, a dining room, and four bedrooms. My ride was equally as blinged out as my crib. People wondered how a guy pushing bootlegs could live so large, but what they failed to realize was my attention to detail is what made my business, and future businesses, flourish. It hasn't stopped. My success is because A to Z matters equally. I'm a perfectionist. I'm so competitive I refuse to lose to anyone, including myself.

Working hard allowed me to play hard. It's something that has carried over through the years. While I was pushing the bootlegging business, I celebrated my birthday one time when Quincy came to town. It was like 2005 or so, and we went to one of my favorite ol school hangout spots in Fayetteville, Chiefs. My reputation was one of a legend there, that was my spot. Everyone from the doorman, to security, to the DJs, to management, and especially the bartenders and waitresses, knew Lamont, or 'Boss', was in the house. They always had a bottle of Moët champagne on ice waiting for me. This birthday bash had tables reserved for 25 of my friends, and I purchased a bottle of Moët for each of them. I showed up with Quincy and a female friend, who just happened to be a pretty cop named Kionna. I brought her along to braid my hair. She was about seven months pregnant so she couldn't participate in the drinking festivities. Now Kionna was more than pretty, she was fine enough that all the men who saw her wanted a piece of the action. But me and Ki were cool, homies for real. We never crossed any lines or anything.

Sidenote: me and Kionna were the best of friends, flirted, maybe hugged or shared an innocent kiss. But we were such good friends it would feel weird to have tried anything further. Now when I met her that wasn't the case. The night I met her there was a pool party in this club and she stole the show. Kionna was bad as hell and every woman in that club who saw her in that bikini envied her and every man desired her, including me. But she was there with her boyfriend, which was an obstacle for all the men there, except me of course. As her and her beau walked to their car I said something to the effect of how she had all the women hating and it made her laugh. Boyfriend was a little tipsy so made the brutal mistake of walking to the car, leaving Kionna and I in conversation. Digits exchanged, and the rest is history.

Anyway, back to the story. We arrived in a long, pearl white stretch Chrysler 300 limo, of course after Q and I had some drinks at the hotel while Kionna braided my cornrows. Sitting outside of the limo for about 30 minutes watching all the people walk in, the manager knocked on the window and said, "Boss we're ready for you".

The lights hit the club entrance, and the DJ stopped the music and said, "Celebrating a real G's birthday let me introduce you to the one and only Boss!" The fellas and ladies parted like the Red Sea as I slid through with the baddest pregnant chick on my arm and a 6'8 450lb mammoth serving as security. Bottles popped, and the parting crowd sways to the beat as the DJ spins the Rick Ross hit, "I'm the biggest boss that you seen thus far," ripples through the air. The night stamped the achievements I orchestrated over the previous few years. It was a long way from babysitting badass kids in schools, applying for food stamps, and eating a can of green beans for dinner. As I exited the club at the night's end with the pregnant friend still on my arm, little did I know my crazy ass ex Pauline was there and she was steaming mad with regret and jealousy.

"I know damn well that's not Lamont's baby," she said as we were walking by.

My antagonistic friend, who's a cop but was a whoop ass chick before wearing the badge, decided to have some fun and responded, "Are you sure?" as she smirked and walked off.

My ex flipped out and had to be restrained. Security removed her from the club. She couldn't handle seeing someone who might be pregnant with my child.

I LOVE THIS GAME

My expectations were never to get to this point. Humbled is an understatement. When the discussion about making a Robeson Rockets Alumni Game & Reunion Dinner first occurred, I wasn't overly excited about putting it together. Don't get me wrong, the Robeson Rockets hold a special place in my heart, and I wouldn't be who I am without success generated from the idea of two Rec League coaches, myself and Chris Rodriguez.

Now, Chris and I met because we both were volunteering as rival Lumberton recreation league coaches. Each year I would run through the competition which included my rival. No matter how bad Chris wanted to beat me, he just always came up short. One day he approached me with the idea of joining forces and creating a summer travel team for these kids that have nothing to do until basketball season rolls back around. It would help keep the ballers from getting into trouble. Thus, the Robeson Rockets were born.

Many kids came up through the Robeson Rockets, and their games were developed by our willingness to get them from tournament to tournament. The organization flourished for almost a decade, and I garnered a record of 375 wins with only 88 losses. Now I'm no Pat Riley or Coach K, but I always knew how to get people motivated to give their best. To find that one thing that makes them tick. Those CD's and DVD's from the flea market financed the organization and created a safe haven for the kids of the county and surrounding areas. Several times a week, we were in the gyms practicing and almost every weekend I would have seven or eight kids piled up into my Suburban.

The committee responsible for putting the dinner celebration together convinced me that the honor was a show of thanks for creating something positive for our area. They wanted to make sure I received my flowers while I was alive.

My Robeson Rockets Win The State Title

Basketball never left me throughout the years. The love of the game kept me competitive during my Navy career and in pickup games as a civilian. I began to want more than playing and thought of how my basketball knowledge and love could give back to the community.

My gift of the gab and identity within the community constantly introduced me to the right people and led me to coach in the Rec League. I coached kids during the summer and fall seasons and successfully got the kids to buy into my coaching philosophy. My teams made it to the championship each year, and the coach standing across the court was Chris Rodriguez. We developed a one-sided rivalry because I always came out on top.

Chris was a good coach but an even wiser man. "Dam-nit,

Lamont, I can't seem to beat you. Let's change it up and start our own program."

It looked like I got in Coach Chris' head so much that he wanted to be part of my team. I couldn't blame him for wanting to see how it was at the top, but after stepping off my pedestal, my mind caught up to Chris' vision. Kids didn't have any summer travel basketball programs in our community and I honestly wasn't familiar with that whole landscape, but playing against competition outside of your area is how to improve your game. Our group picked up most of the players and provided extra transportation to the tournaments. My merchandise sales at the flea markets generated most of the cash necessary for keeping the organization going. We often stopped at the flea market on the way to tournaments to grab some money for gas and food for the kids.

Once, a Lumberton city representative, upon hearing my name come up in several coaching circles, approached me about starting a program sponsored by Project Safe Neighborhoods. I would coach basketball players who may or may not be good enough to make the school team but whose behavioral problems prevented them from participating. The idea was to keep these kids off the streets and guide them toward a more fruitful life. My past as a hot-tempered knucklehead allowed me to relate to many of the kids. Most of the kids wanted discipline but also needed to know that someone cared for them. During my school days, I took the hard-nosed approach I learned from Mrs. Davenport and Ms. Peterken and catered it to fit my coaching and leadership style.

Lumberton would put up the money to run the program, but North Carolina's Governor's Crime Commission would reimburse the city. My team put together the coaches and brought the troubled players together, and everything ran smoothly for two games. But without warning, Lumberton pulled the plug on the funding. We were reaching those kids through basketball and teaching them skills that would save them from the downfalls of their neighborhoods. I demanded answers, but my requests were brushed away without ever receiving a reason for scratching the program. I was livid because I knew it was a mistake. I knew we were making a difference.

Kelani Jacobs was one of the kids on the Project Safe Neighborhood team. Like most kids, Kelani wasn't bad. He only needed an outlet. I was Kelani's disciplinarian but I knew he knew I cared. We loved each other. He would tell me what was going on in his life and seek my advice on many of the rides to his house after practice.

Kelani hung out with a teammate, Steltson, and two other kids one night. They sat in a car outside of a trailer park. They weren't doing anything to bother anyone. The car got sprayed with bullets, Steltson was hit and barely survived in critical condition, but sadly Kelani passed away. The murder took place at the same time practice would've occurred, but Lumberton ensured practice was no longer an option. Going to his funeral, standing at the back of the funeral home staring at the casket, I remember telling Chris I wasn't able to go up there. Chris urged me on and told me we had to. Seeing his young face in that casket and hearing his mom cry out still haunts me to this very day. Kelani's mother gave me a hug and said, "Lani loved you so much. You meant so much to him." She cried on my shoulder. It was so much for me to handle that I don't think I ever properly grieved. There I was again dealing with a death I didn't know how to handle.

Kelani was the first of my basketball kids that lost their life. I honestly lost count after going to about 10 funerals. The grudge I hold toward Lumberton has never gone away. They failed Kelani and many others. I approached one of the city council members years later at a dinner where we were both guest speakers. Although he tried to justify the situation I wasn't hearing it. I just shook my head and let it go before my emotions spilled out.

The Preacher Wife

One of my players from the Rec League and Robeson Rockets had a mother I had known since I was about 12. I had a crush on her years ago, and seeing her brought back those feelings. It had been some time since I had a serious relationship, so I saw something in this woman that appeared to be the right stuff. She was an aspiring preacher, which really didn't fit my standard type, but I was looking for a change. I was tired of running the streets and really just wanted someone who I could trust and live a less stressful life with. I think I was vulnerable. Having a significant other who portrayed a wholesome lifestyle could fix whatever I always found wrong in past relationships. This was the one who could give me peace of mind, or so I thought.

Our courtship lasted only a few seconds before we dove into marital bliss. I thought seeing her devoted to church and knowing her from the past meant I knew her in the present.

We often forget that you can't believe everything people show you, because it's what they don't show you that matters. People who only knew me by reputation, warned me about the Preacher Wife's propensity to date men with pots of gold at the end of the rainbow. Everyone knew my funds were continuously rising, and my living room was big enough to host our wedding, so the future Mrs. Taylor knew I was living pretty decent, at least compared to the average cat in our area. We got married so fast and settled on a honeymoon in the Bahamas. An addiction to relationships placed the red flags in the shadows. There we were in Nassau, enjoying a sunny vacation, when out of the blue, in the middle of the infamous straw market for no apparent reason, the new wife started crying. I didn't have any earthly idea why. No disagreement, no argument, no nothing. Our return to the States earned me the silent treatment for a week and I still didn't know why. I mean we hadn't even been together long enough to have any real problems yet.

I should've taken heed when my parents stopped coming around. They only met Preacher Wife once, and I thought it had to do with the fact they were Jehovah's Witnesses and didn't care for the presence of the church conflict. But you know, we never really know how our parents know what's best for us or why they don't care for certain friends, but admittedly they're usually right. Things spiraled toward misery quickly, and we started counseling, which was more of a double-teamed attack on my manhood. Preacher Wife chose who we went to, and it ended up being her "Preacher Dad."

Each session was about how I was a heathen who was staining the soul of a precious young lady. In reality, I was shown the hypocrisy of a church leader. Preacher Wife shouted praise from the heavens on Sundays but was mean as the devil in the form of a snake and bi-polar as hell away from the church.

The last straw came when Preacher Wife accused me of having an affair with a young lady. History would generally support such accusations, but I was innocent. My past ho-like ways made me knowledgeable about the habits of a cheater, so while I was no angel, I knew my wife had the devil in her. I tried to ignore the signs, but my cousin backed up the truth that my holier than thou on Sunday Preacher Wife was still in a whole side relationship with her ex-husband. To this day I have never let her know I found out, well until now of course. We got along for a few weeks as I tried to figure things out. But little did I know the manipulating spouse of mine had a sinister plan of her own in motion. After working at the club one night, I got home at about 4:30 a.m. Lo and behold this ruthless woman had cleaned me out in the night. She took everything, even taking my bed and leaving the bed rails on blocks. I guess they ran out of time to grab the television. I was shocked. There had been no arguments, no conversations, no anything. In fact when I left for work, her and the kids looked as if they were sleeping just like any other night.

We separated just as fast as we were married, and I coped by throwing little house parties with friends. My moving on only set her off, and she would show up and make threats. Our union made her think she could kick me out of my own house that she moved into. The nerve of this woman! I don't regret any of my past relationships because there were lessons to learn from each, and I couldn't be who I am without them. The toxicity I absorbed damaged my trust for years to come, and to some degree I'm still not healed. I mean, I honestly believe many of the issues I have today regarding trust and loyalty came from my own experiences with betrayal. But on the flip side of honesty, I know I also unleashed my share of damage. We live and learn and teach.

My Joys: Keisha and Quincy

I called the players and parents into the gym to share one of the most important stories from over the years. You see all of my showcase camps end with an All Star game and every kid as well as their parents want their names to be on that list. So I always try to prepare them for the disappointment of not making it. Not just from the director's view, but also as a parent who suffered that same outcome.

"Parents, there is nothing worse than riding home with your child, and they're crying because someone else hurt them. It's a hurtful feeling, and I've felt it too. Watching him cry made me want to cry." I looked them all square in their eyes as I told them my experience with my nephew, Quincy Miller, who I affectionately refer to as my son. "But I didn't cry with him, I decided to hold him account-able for the things he didn't do."

We returned from lunch at the very first showcase I ever took my son to when he was a freshman, so I continued watching him school the supposed more polished players. The days had been full of learning experiences, but Quincy was clearly ahead of the curve. The coaches at the camp planned to announce the all-star selections, which was the event's highlight. Quincy couldn't wait, so he went on to see his name posted on the wall.

Quincy returned, looking upset. "I'm ready to go."

I don't understand what's happening. "What do you mean you're ready to go?"

"Uncle Lamont, I'm ready to go. I didn't make it." "What the hell? What do you mean you didn't make it?"

Politics had never made an appearance until then. How the coaches and directors treated my nephew showed me how the back door looked. We went to the car, and I looked at Quincy as he tried to hide the tears rolling down his face and said, "Remember that time you didn't get back to block that shot? Remember the time you didn't dive on the floor? You have to prove you gave 110% every time you hit the court, and they can't deny you that you're not the best player on the floor." The parents at the camp stared at me. They were starting to understand. "Now, he wasn't trying to hear this." Laughter erupted.

Fast forward years later. We were riding in the back of a limo at the NBA All Star Weekend, enjoying a glass of champagne and he said, "Uncle Lamont we come a long way. Hey, remember the time you took me to my first camp and I didn't make the All Star team and I was crying." We laughed. Then with a straight face he said "Man I should've made that Allstar team!"

"Yes I agree, you lost the battle but won the war. The goal was never and shouldn't be to make a camp All Star team.

You see, you have to ask yourself, how many of those kids that made that All Star team are sitting in the back of a limo and playing in the NBA?"

My Nephew Quincy Guarding His Idol Kevin Durant

****

My marriage to Tasha didn't end well, but our relationship was heaven on earth compared to the brief disaster stint of a second marriage. We remained cordial through the years. Tasha's sister, Nee Nee, had two kids (Keisha and Quincy), and I relished being their Uncle Lamont. In my eyes the kids involved should not be collateral damage of bad relationships so my relationship with the kids never depended on the relationship with the woman. Keisha was my heart. I remember Keisha riding around with Tasha and I, when she was three, singing "Diamonds and Pearls." We felt like her parents. Keisha won my heart and I love her deeply.

When Keisha was seventeen, she would write me letters updating me on school and other things. Whatever she needed, I did my best to supply it. I bought her a cell phone and paid the bill, mainly because I loved hearing from her and that was my baby. She would tell anybody how much she loved her Uncle Lamont.

That all changed when Tasha called me after midnight one evening in 2005 with the most tragic news I had ever heard.

"Lamont, Lamont! It's Keisha. She's been in a car accident, and it's bad."

I booked a flight to Chicago without hesitation and the next morning I was in the sky. Keisha was in critical condition, but at the time the doctors wouldn't allow any of us to see her. I hugged Nee Nee and Tasha and let them know that I wasn't going anywhere. That's my baby. I always admired how strong Nee Nee seemed to be even when I knew she wasn't. Waiting was the only option, so Tasha and I decided to grab a bite and gather our thoughts in the cafeteria. We weren't there long, before Nee Nee called us. "Y'all need to come up to the ICU right now." The doctors informed the family that Keisha's lungs had collapsed and her kidneys were failing. Goodbyes were in order. Tubes hung out of her nose and mouth, and Keisha's petite body had now swelled beyond my weight. The doctors said she might be able to hear us, but there wasn't any way of knowing.

Although I was a total wreck and broken into pieces on the inside, I held my emotions in check to provide a moment of support. "Keisha, I know you wanted to see me, but you didn't have to do all of this to get me here." I smiled while touching her hand. "Listen, Babygirl, I'm here. If the pain is too much to bear and you want to let go, then let go. It's ok. I'm never going to leave you." Although the doctors said she might not hear us, I remember seeing a tear roll down Keisha's cheek. I knew my baby heard me. She was gone an hour later. Losing Keisha killed me in 1,000 different ways. To this day I still can't listen to the track "Diamonds and Pearls" when it appears on my playlist. I just can't do it. I can never hear that song and not think about her in the backseat belting out that song with all the air her little lungs could provide. It's a grief that time will never heal.

I didn't go back to Chicago for the funeral. I couldn't do it. She was the closest person I had ever lost and I know I wasn't mentally able to handle it. I didn't want to see her lying in that funeral home. I just couldn't do it. I didn't want to. I know I have not properly healed from that moment either and to be honest I don't think I ever will.

I received a call from Keisha's little brother, Quincy, in 2007. "Uncle Lamont, all of my friends are drinking, smoking weed, and having babies. Plus, I'm not getting along with my mother. The only thing I want to do is play basketball." Now I hadn't seen Quincy since Keisha passed away. He was barely 5'10 last I saw him, and I never knew he played ball. But I heard the cry for help, so my only concern was saving my nephew from the hardships of North Chicago. After discussing it with Nee Nee and agreeing he needed to be out of Chicago, custody was secured less than two weeks later, and Quincy moved down south with me. He was fourteen at the time, and my mind was blown away when this kid stepped off the plane. Quincy was 6'5 and going into the ninth grade soon, and I knew he was meant to play ball under my tutelage. But first we had some ground rules and the first one was in the airport. Take that durag off and pull them pants up, I'm sure he was like, "this old guy tripping."

As soon as we got to the house I had Quincy write down his goals.

We worked Quincy out at a local college, and it was evident that he had the skills to pay the bills. Quincy could handle that ball with both hands, crossover, and nail the jumper. I enrolled him into Fairmont High School near my home but the only issue I was dealing with was the coaching staff had an old-school mentality. Quincy had guard skills, and just like I knew, Fairmont made him stay in the post and play him at the center position. When I played Quincy on my Robeson Rockets, he played the point guard position for me at times because his size was a problem.

I was by then one of the most prominent camp directors in the country, probably top five overall. I knew what I was doing. There was an opportunity to enroll Quincy at a camp in Greensboro when he was 6'5 and only in ninth grade. My nephew put on a show.

Politics played into Quincy feeling like a failure, but I assured him that he could be the difference in ensuring those feelings never crossed his mind again. We went to work, but Quincy controlled the outcomes of the paths I put him on. We placed him on one of the top AAU teams in the country. The switch from Fairmont to a nationally recognized school, Quality Education Academy led by one of the greatest coaches our area had seen, that played a national schedule increased the level of competition. By his junior year, Quincy was 6'8 and became the number three ranked player in the country at his position. Duke, North Carolina, Kentucky, Georgetown, and many other schools lined up to win the affection of Quincy.

Now anyone who knows me, knows I am a true Duke Blue Devils college basketball fan. So you can imagine how I was feeling while we were sitting in the legendary Coach K's office at Cameron Indoor Stadium. My love for Duke went back to childhood, and visions of Quincy beating the hell out of the Tar Heels excited me beyond belief. Quincy didn't understand the deep-rooted intensity of the Duke and Carolina rivalry.

To give you an idea of how deep this rivalry goes you have to understand it has ruined families and destroyed relationships. One time, while married to Tasha in the late 90's, as I watched the Tarheels defeat my beloved Duke Blue Devils, I was so upset I pulled out my pistol and shot the television. Tasha came out of the back, shook her head, and went back to the bedroom.

Anyway, I couldn't put my desires on him. Coach K courted Quincy. He gave us two tickets to the Duke and Carolina game in Cameron and seated us directly behind the bench. The hype was real. My dream had come true, and I could die happy.

Everyone on the blogs thought Quincy was going to Duke because it had got out I was a Duke fan. But not once did I tell him, hint to him, or try to influence him to go to Duke. Whatever he decided would be his own decision, or so I thought.

This is where I speak of the ugly truth of high school basketball and the Blue Chips dilemma that would happen every day in back rooms. An ugly reality that taught me about the politics of the game and the financial influences involved with recruiting and just how dirty this game could be.

There was a point when Quincy and I did not speak for about a year. It was one of the most painful times in my life. The stinging of betrayal in my heart has left a scar to this day. I allowed him to play his summer ball with a guy named B. Now this guy had a reputation for being a slick, lying, narcissistic, and selfish soul. But he had the gift of the gab that convinced even me he was a victim of jealousy and envy. That he had created a platform for some of the hottest kids in basketball at the time and people will say and do anything to prevent a black man from elevating in this game. He sat in my living room and promised me he would elevate Quincy to another level and help him achieve his dream. I wanted to give my nephew a chance I knew I could not give him. I loved him so much that I was willing to trust the devil, but the devil does what the devil does.

This sheep in wolves clothing was able to convince Quincy and his mom that I was taking money from him intended to help Quincy and keeping it for myself. Anyone who knows me knows that is not even in my character, that I've always had money and the things I wanted and even if I didn't I wouldn't take anyone else's charity. This was done because I was a threat. I had influence at the time in my nephew's decision and I was not willing to play ball. I would never agree to him picking a school, for example, for the payday that is given to guys like B. One day B, Quincy, and his mom all stopped taking my calls. At the time, I had no idea what was happening. I had become the enemy, no longer the gatekeeper. This man had ruined my family. My temper during those times had made me irrational and reverted back to my old thoughts of action. I made a call once again to my cousin in Charlotte.

The hit was in. We were going to make B pay. To this day he has no idea how close he was to being an intended target. I don't think I was in my right mind at the time. I wanted him to pay for taking my only son away from me. It was my current wife, the only rational voice I could trust with my thoughts of violence, who talked me out of doing anything to jeopardize my future. To let it be, no matter how much it hurts, let it be. The pain I endured to see my nephew at the NBA Draft without me was one of the most disappointing feelings I don't think I will ever let go of. I was robbed out of what should have been our moment, our celebration together, our memories, our reward for all the sacrifices we made together and apart. It can never be repeated. I will never have that moment back. There I was, watching it on TV just like everyone else, as if I wasn't there through the hard days, the workouts, the long drives, as if I played no part. I could only be a fan.

Although I was still smiling and extremely happy that he got to live his dream, a part of me died that night. It was the part of me that would give my entire self to someone else. No single act has ever hurt me as much as that night did. The pain and disappointment still exists in me. I cried many days and nights over this situation but I had to eat it. I had to remember that everything happens for a reason and this was the way it was supposed to be written. Now my nephew and I are close again. I love him as much today as I have everyday, even then my love never wavered. I knew he was a kid being taken advantage of. He was influenced to attend a school where there was a deal in place and B's brother, who had become an agent so they could continue to profit off the kids in their program, could be his agent and eventually screw shit up with his non-experience and lack of knowledge. Not to mention their name was mud in the NBA. No one on the professional level gave a damn what the brothers had accomplished on the high school level.

Yes, I held a grudge against B for a long time, but I eventually convinced myself to let it go. That I had to charge it to the game. B wasn't evil. He was just an opportunist. Years later, B attended one of my events where hundreds of kids were there. He and I talked and even though we never mentioned this specific incident we both knew what we both knew. I expressed that I no longer held any animosity towards him. You see I recognized I wouldn't have been able to create this movement to help thousands of parents and players had I not experienced what I had been through with him. I had come to terms that I could not serve my bigger purpose without that situation. There is no GetMeRecruited without B. He offered no apology and I didn't ask for one. I honestly don't think he will admit he did anything wrong, and if he did he probably would explain it as if he had to do what he had to do and it wasn't personal. I get it, now more than ever now that I have been more involved in this industry. It doesn't matter anyway. Now I'm one of the top event directors in the country and I get to be a positive influence and give hope to thousands of young lives. Times had changed.

My nephew elected to sign with Baylor, and I couldn't have been more proud of him. He dreamed of playing college ball and took it upon himself to leave an unhealthy environment to learn what it would take to get him recruited. Quincy helped lead Baylor to the Elite-8 his first year, where they played future NBA All Star Anthony Davis and his eventual NCAA champion Kentucky squad. Those boys on Kentucky's team looked like a hungry NBA roster, so I knew Baylor would be lunch. After one year, Quincy, a Chicago kid, left Baylor and became a second-round NBA pick. My business started when Quincy crossed the stage and shook the NBA Commissioner's hand, and I saw a kid's dream come true. That was a high I would want to feel again even if it was through other people's kids. But I also wanted to give them the knowledge of the game I didn't have, so they wouldn't have to experience the pain I did from the dirty recruiting world.

My Nephew Quincy Serving As My Best Man

Chapter Six

THE EXAMPLE OF CHANGE: BECOMING A SUCCESSFUL, PROUD, BLACK BUSINESS MAN & LEADER

In '98 and '99, a couple came into the rent-to-own store I worked in Camden, SC, called First Choice, and the girl was fine. Her name was Vicki, and my eyes were locked in whenever she appeared. We began flirting, and then the sneaky sexcapades started once a week, sometimes more. Vicki's boyfriend was oblivious. This guy would even invite me to play basketball with him, and I would always say I would be there, but that was so I would know when Vicki would be available to meet.

These link ups led to Vicki getting pregnant, but it wasn't one of those situations where she was only sleeping with me. Vicki was in a great relationship. Her cheating was a hiccup. As far as I could tell he was a great guy, a nice guy for sure. But you know what they say: nice guys finish last. Man this guy didn't deserve this. I knew how bad it would hurt if he found out. But I don't think I cared. Not because I'm heartless, I think it's because the guy who slept with my wife didn't care how much trauma I would carry throughout my life so why should I care? Yeah, I know that's a terrible way to be but that's how you feel when you've become resentful from the pain of betrayal.

Because of the timing, we knew the baby wasn't mine, and we stopped our fling after dodging that bullet. It wasn't long before my connection with Vicki fired up again. Vicki became pregnant for the second time. The first child was about six or seven. This time, Vicki said the baby was mine. Too much was going on for either of us to want the pregnancy to happen. Although separated, my divorce wasn't finalized, and Vicki didn't want to destroy her family. The choice was hard, at least for her because I definitely didn't want a child, but we both agreed an abortion would be best. I drove Vicki to an abortion clinic in Charlotte and gave her the money for the procedure. The facility would not allow me to be present, so I waited in the car until Vicki came out about thirty minutes later. I was surprised the procedure happened so fast.

188

"Lamont, they cross checked the dates, and there's no way the baby is yours. We weren't together at that time."

I asked if she was sure William was the father, and she said absolutely. Relief and joy were the only feelings I had, and I drove Vicki home. A healthy relationship didn't need my interference anymore, so we permanently called it quits. It would be two years later before Vicki hit me up out the blue.

"We need to talk," Vicki said.

A conversation with Vicki hadn't occurred in two years. What on earth could we have to talk about? I enjoyed our time together, but I moved on.

"The baby's yours!" Vicki said.

There was no, "hi, Lamont, it's good to hear your voice," or "let's link up." Vicki dropped a sledgehammer with no warning.

"Hold on, no, remember the clinic and the calendar said it's Williams' baby," I said.

"His job made him do a DNA test. He's not the father, so that leaves you."

My heart started pounding, and my instinct was to find out the truth. Remember I had been to this rodeo before. I ordered a DNA test and headed out to see Vicki and my potential daughter, who was almost two. The results came back a couple of weeks later, and sure enough, I was her father. Time had been lost. I missed her first words, changing her diaper, watching her take her first steps, and so many other things parents get to enjoy. That loss of time creeps into my mind every time I see parents enjoying the process of raising their children. I didn't get that. This also meant building a connection with my daughter would become a slow process. Losing out on those parenting milestones hurt and pissed me off at the same time. I asked Vicki why she lied at that abortion clinic. Getting the procedure was a decision we made together. We could also have decided to keep the child together.

The Misperception Of A CEO

The faint knocking had grown louder as my opened eyes broke through the fog. The clock said 10 a.m. I remembered placing the do not disturb sign on the door, so why were they bothering me? I checked in late for the basketball tournament in Charlotte and spent a few hours out even later, so waking up before necessary meant a bad mood in waiting. The hotel's white female Assistant General Manager and black male employees were at the door.

"Sir, we smell marijuana in the halls, and we're trying to see where it's coming from," she said.

I smelled weed as soon as I entered my hall the previous night, but it was none of my business. Asking me for help wouldn't get to the bottom of the great weed caper at the Fairfield Inn Northlake. Smoking isn't a habit I've ever taken up. I did try it with my friends a few times just to go along. But one night as my friends and I were outside in the parking lot of Rowland's infamous pool hall, we were laughing and talking and the guys were passing around the blunt. Well it got to me, and not being an expert in the proper way to hold the rolled up stogie, I dropped it dead in a puddle of water. Dead silence. Only angry looks. I knew from that night on, smoking weed was not for me.

The hotel knew what kind of car I drove, a beautiful white challenger with the hot rims I named Pearl, and the misperception that my vehicle is what a drug dealer would drive.

"I don't smoke weed or anything else," I said. End of conversation.

They later slid a paper under my door stating that the room was a smoke-free environment and violators would pay a $250 fine. Obviously, the hotel was warning every patron because they were investigating the source of the smoke. No big deal. I crumbled the note up since it didn't pertain to me. I checked out, and the hotel sent me a portfolio with an extra charge of $250. I called my best friend to see if he had received anything since he was at the same hotel. Nothing. He didn't even get the note under the door.

I called the hotel. The Assistant GM made the charge, but she wasn't there. The black gentleman at the desk when I left was on the phone. "Who the hell is she to charge me $250 for smoking when I don't smoke?" I didn't give him a chance to respond. "She never asked to come in to smell for smoke. She never saw anything physical. What about me made her think I was probably the one smoking?" I knew I didn't move or dress like your typical fifty year old or drive what society expects. "You're going to take that charge off, and what is it about me?"

The gentleman said, "I'll go down to the room and see if there's any validity to her claims." He returned and found zero reasons for the Assistant GM to make those charges. He agreed and said that lately she had been trippin'.

I called corporate to give them the information. The Marriott headquarters doesn't like it when their Titanium Elite members are messed with. I wasn't backing down until I received a reason she charged me. The GM of the Charlotte branch reached out to me, and I relayed the same message. I demanded to know why my name was being slandered. My role on a national level could be in jeopardy if parents and coaches perceived me the way those charges detailed my behavior. The work I've done to get here is too crucial to allow people to victimize me without repercussions.

Wiping out the $250 will never justify what that person did to me. My success doesn't make me equal because society attempts to define me by my blackness. They want to claim that hard work, professionalism, and opportunity outweigh or erase the color line, but I'm a black man in America, and they want to make sure I understand that they know exactly who I am to them.

****

Too many people try to make life a black or white thing in America, but you cross the lines and enter the category of racism, which both sides and other colors are guilty of doing. I judge people as people (yes, I see color), and if you're not worth a damn, you're just not worth a damn no matter what color you are, period. Stereotypes are harmful, but you aren't doing yourself any favors if you live up to those preconceived limits attached to your outer image.

I started doing my best not to get labeled as late or un-professional. Brothers and sisters want you to support them because they're black. I agree that support is necessary because society limits how successful black businesses can be and we don't start on the same level playing field. But don't take advantage of my color. Do the work, and I'll be there for you, but you'll eventually fail if I come to you without a just reason.

Be early and start with step one. Mastering the basics of your brand is how you move forward. Ignoring or under-appreciating your customer is how you remain stagnant.

Also, keeping pace with your white competition is a recipe for failure. It's unfortunate, but a black person in America has to be ten times better just to be considered equal. An Ohio coach once said, "good enough is not enough. It is forever the enemy of your very best." Black people need to take that approach if they want their businesses to have longevity.

NATIONWIDE

Jealousy is an interesting thing in life. It never appears when you're perceived as safe. You'll notice competitors pretend to be friends when your name isn't even in the hat but watch how quickly they change when your efforts breed success. It's bad enough when society doesn't want you to have a seat at the table, but it's a different story when your own people scheme to keep you down. The African-American community tends to stay in line with the slave mentality. We have the battle of color with the field slave vs. the house slave. Personal interests keep us wanting to please the master, so we give the secrets of someone else's success or hold onto information that could benefit our counterparts. You rarely see other nationalities battle within the way the black community does.

My team took some early lumps due to a lack of understanding of how we would get pushed. The pressure black men in our position are under in this industry is legit. Losing your composure can cost you everything, and you learn that certain people purposely push you to that point.

One employee got into it with a white parent. This pair was obnoxious and antagonistic. My employee assumed he could handle it himself, a street style pull up, but there's no place for that in business. The kid's parents took us to court, and we were lucky to settle things promptly. A disagreement with an opposing coach turned me into the 'bout it, 'bout it, Lamont. The guy did everything in his power to push my buttons. Some people will risk getting their ass whooped if it means you get discredited. I knew a behind-the-scenes conversation had to happen, but my emotions ran wild. The assistants restrained me as I ripped off my shirt and ran after the other coach. The kids were all watching, but I just didn't care. I was tired of being the nice, professional guy when these basketball guys have no idea that I still have that one hitter quitter. I would be tested in this manner several times in my years at the GetMeRecruited helm.

Coach Isaac Pitts, who was the first coach to believe in Quincy and built his HS career, became pretty close to me over the years, he would be a mentor to me, and eventually, I achieved enough success and respect to be his mentor. We balanced each other out in a competitive world. The best advice I received from Pitts was, "Lamont, it ain't the white folks you have to worry about. It's these niggas you gotta watch. They're going to smile in your face but you have to watch them. The white folks will tell you if they don't like you, but they'll work with you because of the money."

It's rare to see black people watch you go up the ladder and be happy for you. Some of my own people wouldn't look at me as being as good as the white competition when I started out. It broke my heart because the whole reason I even started doing this was for all of us. I wanted to create generational wealth. Some movements were slowed because I learned to keep my guard up based on the betrayal I've encountered in this business.

There was a man named David Kelly who reached out to me and painted a fantastic idea for the EBC (Elevate Basketball Circuit). Teams from all around the country were going to be involved. My growing reputation earned me an invitation to do the head scouting and reporting for the organization, so I participated in all the meetings and became part of the leadership staff. I brought a long-time friend and trainer, Gilbert, along for the ride with the EBC. Changing the narrative of backstabbing and jealousy was something dear to me. I always brought deserving people with me when a good thing happened. When I eat I want my people to eat. We were about to change the landscape of amateur basketball in America. Unfortunately, the second session of EBC fell apart. David Kelly gave too much power to AAU coaches at the door, and they took control of the money. The referees didn't get paid, and the doors were closed on day two. The media went to town on the story, and David mishandled the situation.

Sports Illustrated reached out to me for a response, and an NBC news outlet in New York interviewed me. My involvement never came across as handling money, so there wasn't much for me to do. I went out for a few drinks with the refs and coaches who were part of management the night before the collapse, and we all received a text at the same time from David that read, "This is too much. I'm shutting it down."

Anxiety immediately took over. I had personally convinced teams to participate in the EBC, and they counted on us to follow through on our promises. David Kelly cut off all communication and eliminated outside access by deleting social media accounts and the website. People came from different states to play in the tournament, and the doors were locked, and no reasons were offered. Everyone was left holding the bag and equally distraught. I remember that long ride home from Atlanta after it happened and feeling defeated, like my entire business was being challenged and reputation dragged and there was nothing I could do about it. The single most hurtful part of all this came from my main man, Gilbert. He sent me a text on that ride home that read, "Hey man, may God be with you. I know this is a rough time for you, but because of the heat you are in, can you take my name and logo off your websites." Gilbert was my brother, and I would've gone to bat for him seven days a week. He couldn't even call me. I felt abandoned, like my friend left me when we needed to stand together. My staff can attest to the fact it took me many years to get over the hurt Gilbert inflicted on me that night. Once again I had been betrayed.

We reconciled three years later, and he broke things down for me. He worked for some competitors who said it was best if he disassociated himself from all things EBC, including me. I don't blame Gilbert for choosing his family and livelihood over me, but our friendship deserved a conversation. The common strategies employed to keep us down were pulling strings and pitting us against one another. A phone call could've saved our friendship instead of moving Gilbert to the role of a working acquaintance.

Trey is my Vice President. It was actually he and I, on a basketball trip to Little Rock, Arkansas when we met and came up with the concept to create a scouting service that would bring knowledge to parents and exposure to the kids. Pop is my main scout, but before Pop came on board, a guy named Steve helped introduce me to plenty of people in the business. Steve was a good guy, but he was easily influenced. He helped me get my foot in the door, and I showed him business and basketball knowledge. Giving deserved credit isn't an issue for me, so Steve and another employee were placed in a minimal spotlight. People took notice and gave them more attention than necessary. Before long, Steve and the other person thought they were on my level because that's what competitors were telling them. But the people running their mouths didn't understand how much I did behind the scenes to clean up their mistakes. Their reception in the industry didn't match my presence's notoriety, so they branched out to develop a new company. Steve's venture burned to the ground after three months. He and the other guy aren't players in the basketball world anymore. I really wished

Steve would have stayed. He was a good guy with good basketball knowledge. He just lacked the confidence and I was going to make sure he gained that. But his calling was preaching so I can't be mad at that. He gets to fulfill the passion inside of him now and for that I am happy for him.

My Proud Mother At My Basketball Camp

To get to a higher level, I had to switch things up and develop a different philosophy from the old guard. Every program had a subscription service where the college coaches saw a report detailing our player information. My confidant, Twan, said, "Lamont, if you have the kids, the college coaches will come." My philosophy was developing relationships with the kids instead of catering to the coaches. If I had continued following their rules, it would have taken twice as long to reach a level of success. The game was rigged, so I changed the rules. Too many black-run scouting service startups fizzled out too soon because they tried to use a blueprint never meant for them.

GetMeRecruited Takes Off

Whether it was Ohio, New York, Mississippi, or Alabama, I rented a car and went to every event possible to find the kid nobody knew about and recruit the top talent. I took pictures and wrote reports to put on the GetMeRecruited website. I also used my personal car, which had a big GetMeRecruited decal. It had over 430,000 miles on it by the time it got sold.

The GetMeRecruited Charger

GetMeRecruited's first event was the Super 60 Showdown in Winston-Salem. When we started GetMeRecruited, the national and regional camps were primarily white. Any black camps were small showcases on local levels with local players. We pushed the purpose of supporting our people on and off the court. Coach Isaac Pitts offered his gym for the camp, and some of the best players in the state attended. I took advantage of the support received because Pitts had already told me most of the people would fade away as my company grew. The Tarheel legendary point guard, Phil Ford, was our first ever keynote speaker. Luke Maye (North Carolina) and Dennis Smith Jr. (North Carolina State) came to my first camp, showing that my name had started reaching the players. Steve and I almost fell out before this showcase because he thought we should call it the Super 80 Showdown.

Everyone before us always hosted 80 kids. Dave Telep (San Antonio Spurs) and Rick Lewis (Phenom Hoop Report) had a top 80, and at the time Dave Telep was considered a basketball God in our state. I felt going past 60 kids would produce a watered-down product, and the only way for me to stand out was to be different. My vision worked like a charm, 57 of the 60 campers went on to play college basketball.

Giving Life Advice To NBA Player Dennis Smith Jr. While He Attends A GetMeRecruited Camp

There were a couple of guys who helped me stand out above the rest and that I feel forever indebted to. Ced Canty has the only Nike-run AAU program in our state, Team United, and he stepped up to make life easier. Nike called me because Ced mentioned my name and vouched for me. They wanted to supply the GetMeRecruited uniforms. The news was a blessing, but the process was slow, and I wasn't used to taking my time or waiting until the last minute. Ty White, from Richmond, was with rival Adidas, and he said not to worry because he would supply us (out of his budget) if Nike fell short. The thought behind Ty's offer showed he was a solid dude, but Nike eventually fulfilled the order. I was nobody in Ty's world, but it didn't matter to him, he showed me he was a good stand up guy. He and Ced both will forever have my loyalty.

Rob Taylor from Buckeye Prep Report in Columbus, Ohio, is another scout who went out of his way for me. Rob was the first person to see value in my work and pay me to come to one of his events. He even paid for the hotel stay. For several years I had been traveling on my own dime and sleeping in Super 8 & Motel 6. I would take long naps in my car to avoid having to get another night of lodging. But now, once Rob paid me, there was no turning back. The money didn't matter, Rob could've spent $50 on me, and I would've appreciated him. Rob's belief in me and my work went beyond a paycheck. Rob started paying me to go to his events eight years ago, and even though my worth in the industry is more prominent than ever and I receive payment well beyond my imagination, I respect Rob so much that I've never asked him to increase my fee. That's my OG, and I respect him and his work.

We spoke recently while I was passing through Ohio on a trip. He invited me over for dinner with him and his family. I always try to accept invitations by more experienced guys, not just out of respect, but also because I'm a sponge for knowledge. A lot of these young guys today don't take advantage of the old guys who have the experience. See I pay attention. I know Rob has a wealth of experience and knowledge I can absorb. Sitting on his back patio deck Rob said, "Watching you grow has been a joy and a blessing. You brought innovation. The interviews you did with videos were damn genius. You always separated yourself and kept it professional." It's remarkable for someone like Rob to honor me with his words.

I'm not afraid to do something different if it doesn't degrade our culture. For example, we were the first to wear uniformed black polos and play music during games at our events. The kids can relate to my team because we can hold a conversation with them, and it does not feel fake.

Speaking At The Very First GetMeRecruited Event, The 2014 Super 60 Showdown

Cream Rises To The Top

During the first year of GetMeRecruited, I helped as many people as possible to get my name in industry circles, and I did it for free. The hope was to weed out the fake and form strong bonds with those who remained. My efforts guided me to running a camp for a friend who happened to be friends with Rick Lewis. Now Rick and I have never had any issues personally. In fact we get along pretty good. Everyone expected us to have a rivalry because we were close in what our companies do, but I don't think either one of us cared as much about what the other was doing, like the instigators did. The parents, coaches, and others would try to create tension but rarely did we feed into it. Now I won't lie, I did not like his protégé partner Jaime. He was a fake and a phony and I made no effort to hide how I felt. I knew every time this snake would try to dirty our name, and he's been cursed out by me several times because I just couldn't pretend with him. So anyway my friend who was also friends with Rick needed me to find kids to invite to a west coast camp called Phenom, run by a guy named Joe. No problem, so I thought.

A vacation to Miami with my wife was in order. One morning, we were relaxing when I received a call from a number I didn't recognize, but I answered.

The unknown voice said, "Who the FUCK do you think you are? Do you know who I am? I will fucking destroy you."

Starting at ten with me isn't the best idea, but if you're going to do it, then do it over the phone. "Whoa, who the fuck is this?" I had to excuse myself from the room. "I don't know who the fuck gave you my number or who told you this call would go the way you thought it would, but you picked the right one, and I'll find your ass if you want me to."

The unknown voice, who we now know was Joe, said, "You will find out who I am because I'll destroy you. You won't make it another year."

Five years later, my name holds a little weight across the country, and the company is steadily growing. My phone rang, and I recognized the name from five years prior because I had saved it. The call came through while I was at the library doing school work.

"Yes Joe, what can I help you with?" I asked.

"Hey, Lamont. How ya doing, buddy?" Joe asked. "How's everything going?"

"Doing fine. What can I help you with?" There weren't any pleasantries in my voice.

"I'm just calling to see how you're doing. I see the business is booming!"

These shady backstabbers never show you they're watching, but they pay attention year after year and come crawling when they realize your success is no longer momentary.

"Well, Joe, it's surprising to hear from you, considering the last time we spoke, you said you were going to fucking destroy me."

Joe chuckled. "Lamont, you're still upset about that? It was years ago. Let bygones be bygones."

He's lucky I didn't track him down and beat him with his phone. "I actually can thank you for that because you fueled me even more, to become what I am."

The fake laughter stopped. "That's why I'm calling. Let's work something out where you can become my east coast director. You'll have a nice salary and all that stuff."

Joe pretended to be doing me a favor, but this same lame that called me cussing was now asking me if I wanted a job with him. The nerve. After my years of constant rising, he hadn't figured out that I knew I was that dude. "Joe, with all due respect, I will have to decline."

You have to understand that money and success aren't synonyms of one another. My first three years of GMR (GetMeRecruited) were in the red. I had just started breaking above even when Joe called. An all-staff call occurred after hanging up, and I informed them how white business people dangle money in front of you when you've gone without for some time. Now $75k a year is more than enough to get many of my fellow black people jumping, but I wasn't selling out my business to remain under Joe. One thing I know for sure is I will never be bigger than him if I was working under him. Your worth is more than the dollars someone else tries to attach to your name. Joe's call taught me that they're watching me, and my influence is significant if they're willing to bring me into the fold. I've turned down quite a few people over the years that have made some lucrative offers but money isn't the motivation behind GetMeRecruited.

Now I Have This Platform To Speak

The Nike Elite Youth Basketball League (EYBL) is the largest platform in Amateur Athletic Union (AAU) basketball. The most significant players in the country play on the Nike circuit. Recently, the EYBL outsourced its media credentials to Position Sports, which changed its criteria for getting in. Every year, I went to the EYBL to watch the competition, and suddenly I was banned, but I saw some of my white competitors still got to go. The system cheated me. I was at first angry and told my wife "Screw them, I will just watch the kids play at other events."

She never said a word. She just let me ramble on about how I don't need the EYBL and they knew what they were doing.

She never said a word.

After calming down I started thinking about things. The EYBL is loaded with the best African-American players in the country. If I can't represent the culture at the event, then all those black kids will see is a long row of white faces court side. They will probably think they need a white man's approval to find success. I'm one of the top independent black scouts in the country, and the kids that come through my camps know that GetMeRecruited is a Lamont Taylor business and not part of the Nike, Under Armor, or Adidas brands. It mattered more to me that those kids saw someone who looked like them representing the sport without dribbling a ball. That they can be successful in other fields associated with sports.

I swallowed my pride and moved to get back in the EYBL by calling a black executive at Nike headquarters in Oregon I knew. He got me the credentials and upgraded them. If you look at the video or photos, you'll see I'm stationed at halfcourt with about 15 white guys on either side of me.

Phenom Hoops in North Carolina was run by Rick Lewis and Jamie Shaw. They were the top dogs in North Carolina. Rick got Phenom from Joe Keller, and Rick's event was the first we as a GetMeRecruited staff attended. As I stated earlier, I've always liked and respected Rick. Of course, he, just like everyone else, was nice to me when GetMeRecruited was just getting off the ground. I wasn't a threat so I didn't register on Rick's radar, or anyone's for that matter. But yet when North Carolina's basketball "God", Dave Telep, decided to move on to a job with the San Antonio Spurs, he passed the baton to Rick Lewis, so I'm sure many thought we would not survive. Now I liked Dave, and still do, but I'm pretty sure that passing of the guard was only because we weren't expected to survive.

Jamie Shaw was cool initially, but he was one of those privileged preppy guys who didn't play the game but had opportunities gifted to him. Jamie was out of pocket a lot and needed to be checked. He commented about the "hood", and   I said, "Jamie, that's not your forte. You went to Myrtle Beach High School." Jamie dug under my skin with each passing day. If I presented myself in gym clothes and slides while delivering reports, my colleagues would think I was unprofessional. Jamie can do the exact same thing, and they'll say he's just chilling today. That was my reality. Always being judged by a different jury than my peers.

Many people in the industry take a relaxed approach to the day, but I remind my staff that their blackness doesn't afford them the same luxuries. I promoted #raisethebar and #raisethestandard because we couldn't stop moving forward. My approach to all scouting and camp business facets forced Rick Lewis and Phenom to get on our level. I became the standard when Phenom was still on top. We do things that are more than basketball. It wasn't a competition but if we are going to be in the same industry I'm going to force you to be your best and on your toes because that's what I'm going to do even if there was no one else. I'm hoping Rick and I can do an event together some day. It would be good for the state of North Carolina.

I'm the type of guy who can smile in your face and laugh with you but can't stand your ass. That's because if they know how I feel about them or them about me, they will switch it up on me. This way they're comfortable and will continue to do things the same way because they think I don't know any better. My wife finds it quite impressive because how she feels shows on her face from the moment she feels it. If my wife doesn't like you, you'll know in less than a minute. Jamie was one person who I couldn't pretend around. A friend of mine, Steve Mims, tells this story better than I do, but here goes.

Jamie, Steve, and another scout Charles Clark were all in the gym watching games when I entered. As I walk by Steve and Charles both say wassup. I speak back. But then Jamie shouts, "Hey, Lamont! How's it going?"

Lord knows I try. I've come a long way from that guy who used to fight and cuss you out for any little reason. I stopped when I heard Jamie's voice and slowly looked back. "You know I don't fuck with you." And I walked off. Part of my problem with Jamie stems from meeting him during the beginning stages of my business. I didn't mess with many people, so getting to know me was difficult. Any slight disrespect would send me your way for a verbal altercation. I had to learn to scale back and choose my battles wisely. Other scouting services quickly learned that GMR was a formidable competitor. They scheduled events based on our event schedule dates in order to try and steal recruits from my camps, but they couldn't compete with the big dog. To know me is to understand I'm built differently. GMR has operated for the first six out of ten years while I'm in college. I've written papers in-between games while sitting in the gym, in hotel rooms, etc. In a few months I will have completed my doctorate degree. The success is worth it. We now have 43 states, and players from Canada, Bahamas, Jamaica, and Australia that have had players come to GMR camps.

I Speak Because I Have A Platform To Reach So Many

Events take months to prepare, so if anything goes wrong it hits hard. Being a perfectionist doesn't help the cause or my anxiety but it is what it is and I've accepted it. We were in the path of a hurricane one time. Everything with the camps is paid in advance, so canceling at the last minute is catastrophic, considering the bills are always paid in advance in my regime. My team watched the hurricane for days, and we held off calling the event off because of the financial disasters in-store. We had 125 kids registered, and 122 of them still showed up. One of the parents said my influence must be high-level for those families to show up during a hurricane. I never really thought about it before that moment, but as I thought about it yea, we must be doing something right that people can believe in.

Families know we will be there for them, and my team cares as much as I do. They know I'm going to push the campers and my staff to be better.

Pop never really believed he could be anything in life because his family told him that. His nickname used to be Mr. Unprofessional. Pop hated it, but he was so rough in the beginning. We trained him to become more polished, and now he coaches and teaches at a school. He's nowhere near where he needs to be, but he's definitely closer. Trey probably takes more heat than anyone, but I'm grooming him to take over when I'm gone, or at least further in the background. Trey will run the operations. It's important to have people you can trust. My team knows they have a leader who grinds 24/7. I work on problems at 4:00 am because sleep has to wait.

Trying To Teach A Skillset And Pass On A Legacy To Young Brothers Like Pop

Future Goals, What Could've Been and Legacy

Listen, I don't get impressed by much. That's always been who I am. But this guy used to lace them up and fly through the air with unmatched athleticism. Michael Jordan is one of the people who managed to impress the hell out of me. The other guy became President. I watched election night when Barack Obama won. Seeing Jesse Jackson cry caused me to cry, and I can't explain why. But watching the celebration of President Barack Obama was one of the proudest moments I've ever experienced as an American. It's hard to watch how our country has reverted back to hate since Obama left office. We need to come together. Michael Jordan provides more than basketball. He has that it-factor that Kobe adopted from him. He doesn't settle for less. That beat you because I can't allow myself to lose is what I got from watching Jordan.

It's something I can't turn off, and it causes me to be great at what I do. MJ is the ultimate competitor, and I'm the same way with GMR. Problems get fixed.

Reflecting On Life In The Bahamas

The greatness that has turned into GMR can't stop me from wanting more. Entrepreneur dreams have been with me from my early years, and I always push and search for the next thing. Chicago had a nightclub called The Click, and all of the Chicago celebrities at the time like Da Brat, R. Kelly, Kanye West, and a gang of others used to go there. You could see a coat-check area and a live band area when you walked into The Click. Live jazz circulated through the site, giving off a lounge vibe. The other side of the club hosted a comedy club. Upstairs was the actual club party area. There was loud hip- hop blasting, and the dance floors were packed with a lot of grinding happening.

Four bars provided a space for everyone to have a drink. I love comedy clubs and r&b music. There's a need for a black business to host black comics, so the vision is the next thing to come from my business skill set.

I am a college-educated black man, and it's something to be proud of. So many of us don't believe we have the opportunity to strive for such awesomeness. I know the Navy entered my life right out of high school, but there was a deep desire to attend an HBCU. I loved watching *A Different World* and often wondered what it would be like to hang out with Dewayne Wayne or listen to Whitley Gilbert talk. Ron could've been my misunderstood sidekick. Hillman College would be my life, and I would've embraced every black moment.

I didn't go to an HBCU, but I made sure that college is part of my story when it's all said and done. A legacy is memorable and positive. People will look back and see I cared about many people, and moves were made to improve my circumstances because I wanted the ability to do the same for others. My struggles helped me understand the low moments of others. I prayed to God and promised that if he pulled me from the darkness, I would change my life and be a better person. I still went left when I should've gone right, and I pulled more women than I should've, but I tried to do more good than not. Sometimes in life we just get lucky. That's how I felt when I met my current girlfriend. She's a different breed. She's restored my faith in knowing there are good women out there who are not tempted by infidelity. Who will hold me responsible for not being the best version of me. Who will not allow me to wreck my life over a silly decision. You see I can't get away with the stuff I used to do because she's not with any of the shits. Her small Georgia town with the dirt road background created a goal-oriented no nonsense queen. She's an inspiration to anyone who comes across her. She's a pro- black woman with that black girl magic naturally instilled in her. Our personalities are different. She keeps me grounded.

She taught me how to have fun in the club without popping bottles.

How we met is not one of fairy tales. It was a chance meeting of two people who really weren't in the mood to be in the very place they would meet their soulmate. When my wife met me I had cornrows and was sippin' out of a bottle of Moet at that same club, Chiefs. Her sister dragged her out of the house on a rainy night because she was dating one of security. I was single and had no desire to leave the house and drive 45 mins in the rain to this spot. But something moved me to do so. Maybe it was divine intervention, maybe it was destiny. What I do know is that it was supposed to happen. I earned this happiness. I paid my dues. I had endured enough meaningless sexual episodes. I had been a part of toxic relationships. One of the best days in my life was when I married Tasha Taylor. No, it's not my first wife Tasha. Ironically both my first wife and my wife now share the same name, but they are two totally different people to me. One is a part of my past and the other is helping me build my future.

Tasha And I Wedding Photo

There's one other day I'm extremely proud of, it's the day I shared the stage with my wife as we received our master's degrees the same day in DC. I've learned how to button up my shirt straight and pay attention to the little things in marriage as I do with my business. Her love was an obtainable goal that I waited too long to chase. And although no marriage is perfect. No marriage is without its trying days. There is a feeling you get when you know you are with the woman you were intended to be with, and man it feels good.

Tasha And I Graduation Receiving Our Master's Degrees

We are not only thankful for each other but we are also thankful for our daughters. Her two biological daughters, Laila and Kyra, and my biological daughter, Ayanna. We have somehow managed to break the stereotype that blended families are difficult and have made it work graciously. Many families end up with resentment, jealousy, separation, etc, but I am so happy I have not had to experience that. They all love and support each other and get along great. That makes me happy, and that is all I want. I love them. They love me. Those are my girls.

Fun day at the water park with my daughters Kyra, Ayanna, and Laila.

I've gone through so many sleepless nights. Nights of uncontrollable pain and embarrassment. But I made it. I made it so you can make it. This is the open book to my life. Writing this book has been therapeutic. It has given me the opportunity to forgive myself. To love myself. This book is me.

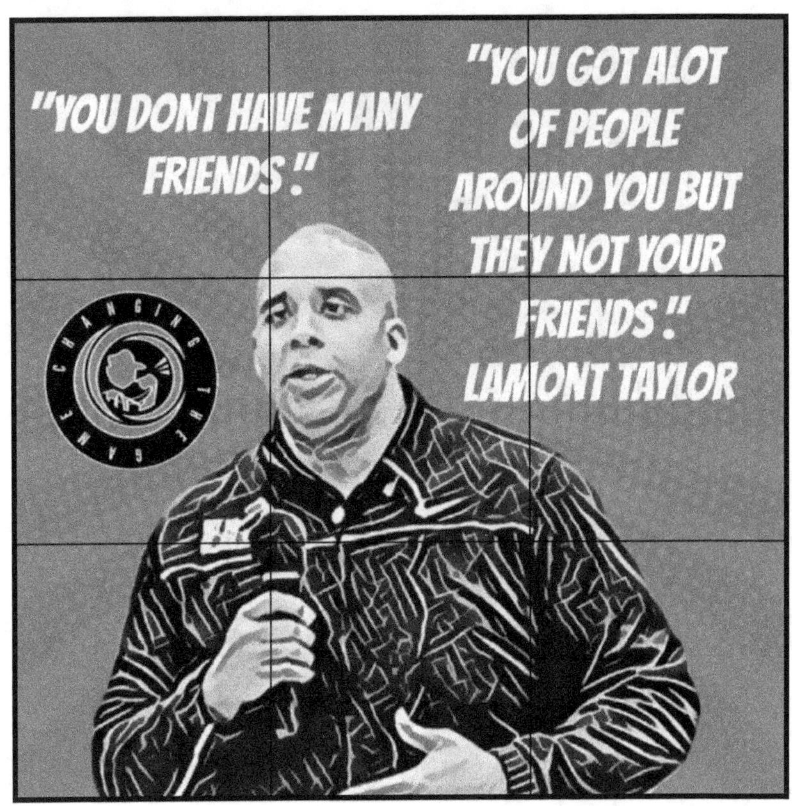

Changing The Game Life Coach

About The Author

LAMONT TAYLOR

Who is Lamont Taylor?

He's the successful and nationally recognized CEO/President of GetMeRecruited, a national basketball scouting service. His mission is and always has been to motivate and help others grow into their purpose, in all walks of life. The International Coaching Federation (ICF) accredited life coach and motivational speaker believes everyone can find success in life, if they don't settle for less than they deserve. The only child of Willie and Irene Taylor continues to prove you can rise above your circumstances and break away from the systemic chains of mental oppression. Lamont is a former U.S. Navy sailor with a BS in Psychology and an MBA in General Business. He is currently finishing up his Doctorate in Leadership requirements.

The proud son, husband, and father would like to thank everyone who believed in him, mentored him, and especially those who thought the hard-headed, chubby kid from Brooklyn, New York and Lumberton, North Carolina would never find his way in life.

The purpose of this book is to give everyone insight into this unconventional journey of my life. The hurt I caused, the pain I endured, the burdens I carried, the accolades I achieved, the failures I experienced, the sincerity of my heart, the reasons at times I seemed heartless, the reckless behavior I displayed, the people I disappointed, the joys of success, the lows of my depression, the love I gave out, the love I embraced. All of these contributed to who I am because this book speaks about who I was.

I sincerely apologize to some of the people who may be hurt by certain parts of this book, but I hope you will forgive me for telling my truth, for releasing the restraints of events that have been held hostage in my soul, my entire life. This book is not intended to hurt or embarrass anyone, especially those closest to me. It is to show you I made it despite my circumstances. I chose to keep pushing forward until I found my passion and my purpose.

When you finish this book you will understand not everything that glitters has always glittered and hopefully you will be truly inspired to believe, that if this guy can become a CEO, a family man, and a devoted husband, then damn near anybody can. One thing I've learned throughout my journey is growth. I would not be who I am if I had remained who I was. I had to grow mentally. I had to allow myself to try.

Trust my instincts, my talents, and not overthink. The 'how' is never as important as the 'why.' You will never know how far you can go unless you're willing to risk going too far. I hope you enjoy an intimate and raw look into my autobiography, "I Am Who I Am Because I'm Not Who I Was."

Speaking to a news reporter in Nassau, Bahamas

I Love To Speak To The Masses

The Weight Of The World On My Shoulders

Flaunting Pearl On South Beach

My Driver Awaiting My Arrival In The Bahamas

Speaking To A Group Of Athletes In Jamaica

Acknowledgements

(PEOPLE WHO I LOVE, SUPPORTED ME, INSPIRED ME, OR ENCOURAGED ME ALONG THE WAY)

9th Wonder

Aaron Robinson

Alexis Andrews

Andre Gray

Aneisha Scott

Anthony Bruton

Anthony Davis

Anthony George

Antwan Fletcher

Arne Morris

Banner Demers

Beverly Silva

Bobby McCallum

Brian Dawson

Brian George

Bryan Markley

Bryce Lanning

Cedric Cornelius

Chris Myatt

Chris Rodriguez

Clairdell McCallum

Craig McLamb

Crystal Moore

Cybrena Davis

Dameon Key

Dave Brown

David Lowery

Denykco Bowles

Dexter Salmon

Diane McCallum

Donyell Bryant

Dwayne West

Ellisha Griffith

Eric Johnson

George Foxwell

Gerard McCrae

Glenn McCallum

Gloria Allen

Heather Bain

Heather Seibles

Howard McQuaige

Hubert Pearson

James Veal

Jasmine Jones

Jason Jordan

Jeff Dudley

John Kinsman

Johnny Silver

Jonathan Mcleod

Jordan Turnmire

Kendrick Williams

Keysha Bailey

Lamont Morgan

Lavander Ford

LeVelle Moton

Linda Serrano

Lolita Frazier

Mark Watson

Mary Davenport

Mary Shipman

Matisha George

Maurice George

Mel George

Melvin Williams

Mike McRae

Nichole Collins

Nicole Sampson

Percell Cobb

Percy Wright

Quincy Reddick

Rasheena Graham

Rick Lewis

Rob Taylor

Robert Cobb

Savannah Mack

Shawn "OG" McRae

Shawn Bethea

Stargell Love

Stephon McQueen

Steve Mims

Tasha Moody

Tiffani Weathers

Tiffany Clifton

Tim Fields

Timmy Clark

Tony Squire

Vanessa Taylor

Vonnie Holliday

Walter Steele

Will Stanley

Please forgive me if you were inadvertently left off…..

I Love You All!

My mother proudly wearing my brand